THE STANLEY CUP

THE
STANLEY
CUP

JOSEPH ROMAIN and JAMES DUPLACEY

B. Mitchell

CONTENTS

This edition published by
W H Smith Publishers,
 Canada

Produced by
Bison Books Ltd.
Kimbolton House
117 A Fulham Road
London SW3 6RL

Copyright © 1989 Bison
 Books Ltd.

ISBN 0-88665-578-1

Printed in Hong Kong

PAGE 1: *The Greatest Comeback: The Toronto Maple Leafs of 1942 lost the first three games of the finals before coming back to win the last four in dramatic fashion. Here, Pete Langelle (8) has just fired the winning marker in game seven. Bob Goldham and Gaye Stewart are the stick-waving celebrants, while Mud Bruneteau (9) and Carl Liscombe are the dejected Wings in the crease.*

PREVIOUS PAGES: *Bobby Orr in full flight. Orr led the Bruins to Cup wins in 1970 and 1972, becoming the first two-time winner of the Conn Smythe Trophy.*

INTRODUCTION

The glittering prize of the National Hockey League, the Stanley Cup, rotates on its dais at the Hockey Hall of Fame, capturing the awe and imagination of all who visit the shrine to winter's finest sport.

Lord Stanley's gift to sport is the best-known by far, but it was neither the first, nor the only, award offered by a Governor-General to support fledgling sports in the Dominion of Canada. The *Montreal Gazette* of 1876 reported that Lord Dufferin offered a prize to winners of a local hockey tournament. In 1909 the Earl of Grey gave his silver bowl, and his name, to the premier trophy for Canadian football.

In the very early days, the Dominion Hockey Challenge Cup (as Stanley's Cup was known in 1893) was skated for not by elite, well-paid professional athletes, but by bankers, engineers and students whose weekends were devoted to playing the new game that was sweeping the nation. Though the game was played by part-time amateurs in Montreal, Ottawa and Toronto, the rapid and widespread acceptance of the Montreal rules made it clear that the new sport had consistency and a bright future. Stanley created the award to foster the growth of what he saw as an important Canadian invention – a new sport called ice hockey.

P.D. Ross, an upstanding member of the Civil Service and aide to Lord Stanley, was an active player and booster of the game. It was largely Ross who fostered the Governor's interest in the sport. He and Lord Stanley saw that the donation of a trophy to be played for by 'people who matter' would provide a focus for the teams and leagues around the country.

Lord Stanley could not have begun to imagine how right he had been. Today, in a nation of 26 million people, one would be hard-pressed to find one who was ignorant of the Cup and its significance. In fact, though Canada still acknowledges the Governor-General as the head of state, more people would know who won the Cup last year than would know the name of the current Governor-General (Madame Jeanne Sauve).

OPPOSITE: *Wayne Gretzky lofts the Cup after Edmonton defeated*   *Philadelphia in game seven on 31 May 1987.*   TOP: *Bruin Ray Bourque (77) puts the wrap on*   *Oiler Esa Tikkanen, Cup finals, 1988.*

INTRODUCTION

RIGHT: *Lord Stanley of Preston. Lord Stanley, Governor-General of Canada, donated the Dominion Hockey Challenge Cup in 1893. The silverware that today bears his name is the oldest trophy competed for by athletes and is symbolic of professional hockey supremacy.*

OPPOSITE: *The original Stanley Cup. Retired in 1970, the original 'Mug' now rests at the Hockey Hall of Fame and Museum in Toronto. The Stanley Cup now in use was painstakingly recreated from its predecessor, using the same silversmithing techniques as in Lord Stanley's day. The Cup itself has had numerous changes in size and shape; it has been beaten, kicked, stolen and lost but it still remains the most noteworthy prize in the history of the game.*

The pride of the National Hockey League began as a challenge trophy. Teams representing any league could play for it. Team members only had to convince the Trustees that they were worthy opponents willing to abide by the rules, and a challenge would be set up. In the first 30 years of the Cup's existence, there were 53 such challenges. The Cup was coveted by teams from towns and cities ranging from Sydney, Nova Scotia to Victoria, British Columbia, and every whistle stop in between.

Prestigious as it was, and is, the Stanley Cup has almost never been handled as an *objet d'art*. It seems that the only time the Cup is safe is when it is perched on its turntable at the Hockey Hall of Fame in Toronto. It has been left behind at the photographer's studio, forgotten on a cold and lonely midnight highway, kicked into the Rideau Canal, and roughly mended in an Edmonton auto body shop. At the Hall of Fame, it is polished with care and displayed carefully in its sealed glass case. Yet those godlike men who sweat and bleed for it hurl the Cup about and parade it with a gusto that gives Lord Stanley's bowl that magic sparkle no polish could create.

Today, the Stanley Cup playoffs are a glitzy, professional event. The opposing sides maintain a very even and consistently high level of play and the atmosphere is electrifying. However, in the bygone days of Cup challenges, things were a bit different, to say the least.

INTRODUCTION

ABOVE: *Denis Potvin (5) and Mark Messier (11). Potvin was the first player selected in the 1973 NHL amateur draft, and the New York Islanders built their franchise around him. He won the Norris Trophy in 1976, 1978 and 1979 and was a seven time All-Star. He also holds NHL career records for goals, assists, and points by a defenceman. His record for playoff games (185) was surpassed by Canadien Larry Robinson in 1989. Mark Messier has been an integral part of the four Cup-winning Oiler teams, and was named captain of the team following the Wayne Gretzky trade in the summer of 1988.*

In 1905, in Dawson City, Yukon there lived a successful entrepreneur named Joe Boyle. The robust and boastful chairman of the Dawson Athletic Club, he was the natural leader of the local contingent bent on winning the Cup from the southerners in Ottawa. Boyle, a businessman with contacts in Ottawa, put together the deal and the finances which brought the Yukon Nuggets to Dey's Rink in Ottawa. The unevenness of play was so evident – Ottawa outscored them 32-4 – that the Trustees were forced to introduce fairly stiff rules about who could get to Stanley Cup ice. They brought forth a playoff system whereby all challengers would play down to one solid contender, ensuring no repeat performances of the 1905 Dawson fiasco. Back in the Klondike, they were licking their wounds and smouldering with plans for their own trophy, one to be forged out of rich Yukon gold.

During the heyday of the Pacific Coast Hockey Association (1912-24), the level of play between West and East was fairly even, since most of the western players were coaxed out of eastern rosters. The league officials, however, were such innovators where the rules were concerned that there were disputes over what brand of hockey was to be played. So great were the problems that there was even hot debate over whether six or seven men would be allowed to skate. Although the rulebook went through some hard times, Cup play continued to have a unifying influence at the grass roots level in Canada. It was during this time that the first American teams competed for and won the Stanley Cup. In 1917, the Seattle Metropolitans became the first winners of the Cup to hail from the United States.

In 1919, the playoffs yielded no winner. The great flu epidemic of that year took its

toll on the sporting world, and so many players fell ill that the competition had to be cancelled. The Montreal Canadiens team was very badly shaken when Joe Hall, their star defenceman and long-time friend, died as the result of illness.

In 1926, the Stanley Cup came under the control of the National Hockey League, where it has remained to date. In that year, the Western Hockey League gave up the ghost, leaving the healthy and expanding NHL as the only remaining major league. Other leagues have come and gone, but none has produced a team which was seen as a convincing challenger.

Since 1947, the NHL has had an arrangement with the Stanley Cup Trustees which has ensured that the NHL would be in a position to determine the conditions of competition for the Cup. The exact wording of the agreement is confidential, of course, but it makes it clear that the NHL is in control of the situation.

In 1952, the Cleveland franchise of the American Hockey League applied for a franchise in the NHL. Jim Hendy and his colleagues thought they had a team with sufficient talent to join the Big Six. They may have had the team, but the NHL Board of Governors decided that Hendy and company did not have the financial resources necessary to qualify. The following October, Jim Hendy sent a letter challenging the NHL to play his Cleveland Barons for the Stanley Cup, providing that Cleveland won the AHL title. The NHL response was rapid and crushing. They declined on two counts: Firstly, Cleveland had not yet won the league title, thereby making the challenge a little hollow; and secondly, the Stanley Cup was reserved for challenges between major league teams, and Cleveland did not qualify.

ABOVE: *Waving the Towel: Vancouver became the sixth expansion team to reach the finals in 1982, only to be swept by the NY Islanders. Their fans, following the example of coach Roger Neilson, began waving the 'white flag' of surrender whenever a referee's call went against their team. Of the original six expansion teams, only Pittsburgh and Los Angeles (the Oakland franchise folded) have yet to reach the ultimate peak of franchise glory, but with Mario Lemieux in Pittsburgh and Wayne Gretzky in LA, their futures look bright.*

INTRODUCTION

RIGHT: *The Old Chebuctos of 1888, including (top row, far left) J.G.H. Creighton, the man often credited with writing the first rules for hockey.*

BELOW: *The Yukon Nuggets travelled by foot, dogsled, ship and train to challenge for the Cup in 1905. After the 4000-mile trek the team, out of energy and almost out of money, lost in straight games to Ottawa, outscored by a 32-4 count.*

BELOW RIGHT: *The barrel of the modern Stanley Cup, featuring the names of players and officials for each winning team. The Cup was changed following the 1947 season from an elongated cigar shape to the barrel shape still in use.*

During the period of the six-team league, the powerhouses took turns building Stanley Cup dynasties. In the 20 years following World War II, Toronto, Montreal and Detroit shared the glory in all years except 1961, when Chicago jumped to the winner's circle for one brief season. The Stanley Cup came to represent the undisputed pinnacle of winter sports achievement. The annual event brought families around the radio or television to share in the exciting drama of Stanley Cup hockey.

Through expansion, Lord Stanley's influence began to be felt in the United States. Philadelphia's achievement in 1974 gave notice that the newcomers to the NHL had

opened up the field. Later that decade, the New York Islanders dynasty silenced even the harshest critics. A new era of hockey had been launched, and it would be every bit as exciting as it was in those days gone by.

Today, there are 21 teams in competition for the Cup, and all of them hail from familiar places. Over the years, though, teams from hither and yon have skated for the big hockey prize. They have come from places like Halifax, Rat Portage, Renfrew, Galt, Kingston, Sydney Mines, Portland, Seattle, Victoria, Cobalt, Cornwall and Haileybury. In all, teams from 17 leagues have become the Stanley Cup champions, and many other leagues have sent unsuccessful challengers.

Throughout the history of the Stanley Cup, the city that gave birth to the game in 1875 has towered above the rest: Montreal fans have seen no less than six different teams surface as Cup champions, and have won more than twice as many Cups as the nearest rival city.

In 1902, in northern Michigan, a Hall of Famer by the name of Doc Gibson organised the first professional hockey league. When the upstart pros offered a challenge for the Cup, the Trustees declined the offer, fearing that the Dominion Hockey Challenge Cup might be taken out of the Dominion. But since 1917 American cities have been hot contenders for the treasured silverware and have been more successful than anyone at the turn of the century could have imagined possible.

Today's Cup Trustees, Brian F. O'Neill and Justice Willard Estee, continue the tradition as final arbiters in Stanley Cup play. Justice Estee functions in a ceremonial way, whereas Mr. O'Neill operates in a very concrete manner as NHL vice-president of administration and the final authority in disputes. The attention of millions of people around the world is focussed each spring on this oldest of North American trophies, and this long-standing tradition never fails to electrify all who come into contact with it.

The Stanley Cup spends most of its time reflecting the mesmerized faces of visitors to the Hall of Fame. Most of them know little or nothing of its rich history, but still they are drawn to this silver dynamo. The casual fan and the devotee alike are spellbound by this focus of tremendous human energy: They marvel to see names they heard from their fathers, and they imagine games yet to be played.

ABOVE: *Dawson City was a prosperous Yukon mining town in 1900, and hockey was a popular pastime. The idea of a Stanley Cup challenge began here and reached fruition in 1905. It was the dream of entrepreneur 'Klondike' Joe Boyle to challenge for the Cup, and after his rag-tag team won the Yukon championship in 1904, he felt he had the troops to complete the feat. Their journey lasted 24 days, cost $6000, and as history tells us, produced the most lopsided defeat in Stanley Cup history.*

1893

Montreal AAA (AHA)

Prior to Lord Stanley's donation of the Dominion Hockey Challenge Cup, later known as the Stanley Cup, a variety of formal and informal organisations were competing for a number of trophies. Chief among these was the Senior Amateur Trophy, which was the prize of the Amateur Hockey Association since its formation in Montreal in 1886. By 1893, three Montreal teams (the Victorias, the Crystals, and the Montreal Amateur Athletic Association), The Quebec Hockey Club and the Ottawa Hockey Club (the Generals) comprised the AHA, today regarded as the premier league of that time.

As the champions of the Amateur Hockey Association, and claimants to the Senior Amateur Trophy, the Montreal AAA were awarded the Stanley Cup in 1893, and were therefore required to accept any challenges for the Bowl. However, no team challenged the AAA for the new treasure, and they remained uncontested Stanley Cup champions until the end of the following season.

Haviland Routh was the outstanding scorer of this first Cup season, scoring 12 goals in 7 games. Billy Barlow, also of Montreal AAA, was also a star of the season, scoring 7 goals in 7 games. Frank Stocking, a stand-in goaltender for Quebec's final game, allowed 14 goals in this game, and it is somewhat ironic that he is credited with the first plans for a standardized goal net.

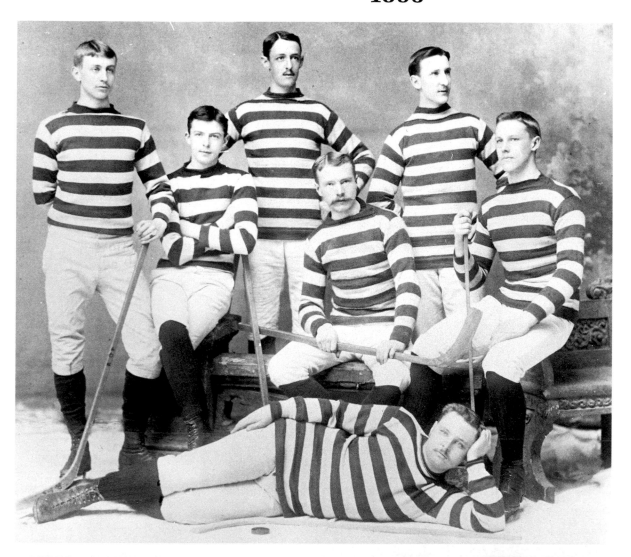

PREVIOUS PAGES: *The New York Rangers congratulate the Boston Bruins after the Beantowners' Stanley Cup win on 11 May 1972. Phil Esposito (7) and Johnny McKenzie (19) lead the procession for the Bruins.*

OPPOSITE TOP: *Prior to the introduction of the Stanley Cup, the Senior Amateur Trophy was the premier prize of the hockey season.*

OPPOSITE BOTTOM: *The Victoria Rink in Montreal was the birthplace of hockey. Here the Montreal AAA play the Victorias in the 1890s.*

ABOVE LEFT: *Frank Stocking (far left) is seen here with the 1893 Quebec intermediate squad.*

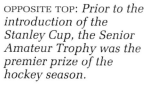

LEFT: *The Eastern Champion Montreal AAA of 1889. The 'Winged Wheels' would go on winning and become the first Stanley Cup champions in 1893.*

1894

Montreal AAA (AHA)

Hall of Famers Harvey Pulford (Ottawa) and Mike Grant (Victorias) made their first of many outstanding appearances in Stanley Cup play in 1894. However, when the ice had cleared, neither would scratch his name on the Cup that year.

The Amateur Hockey Association's regular season ended with four of the five competing teams tied for first place. This created headaches for league officials. Some sort of playoff system had to be established to decide the league titlists. As thousands of people came out to hockey matches there was considerable money to be made in hosting regular games, let alone these first 'playoff' matches. Meetings were held to determine the playoff system, and representatives from Quebec, Ottawa, Montreal AAA and Victorias argued their cases. The strongest voices contended that the playoffs should be held in Montreal, but the Quebec contingent was in strong disagreement, and withdrew from the series. In return for a guaranteed shot at the Crown, Ottawa agreed to allow all games to be played in Montreal. This complicated scenario led to the playing of the first intra-league playoff series.

In a winner-take-all match, the defending champions defeated their cross-town rivals, the Victorias, 3-2, setting up the final encounter with the Ottawa Capitals. Billy Barlow of Montreal scored twice, including the decisive marker, as the AAA skated off with a 3-1 victory and their second Stanley Cup victory in as many Cup seasons.

ABOVE: *The dapper P.D. Ross (back row, left) presided over the Ottawa club he hoped would win the first Stanley Cup. Ross seldom receives the credit he is due for being so instrumental in persuading the Governor-General to donate the Cup. Ross's team never did win the Bowl.*

RIGHT: *Montreal AAA of 1894 featured Hall of Famers Haviland Routh (top row, second from right) and Billy Barlow (middle row, second from right).*

1895

Montreal Victorias (AHA)

Things did not get any easier for league officials in 1895. In fact, the season's end left such a complicated muddle, it is difficult to make any sense of the conundrum which led to the Montreal Victorias' possession of the Cup.

Prior to completion of the AHA season, the omnipotent Cup Trustees, Sheriff John Sweetland and Philip D. Ross, had accepted the challenge of the Queens University team from Kingston, Ontario. They ordered that Montreal AAA would defend the title on 9 March. On 8 March, however, the AHA season ended, with the Victorias on top. As regular season champions, the Montreal Victorias naturally assumed that they were entitled to defence of the Cup. Due to the rules establishing the Cup as a challenge trophy, the Trustees believed that AAA held the title until all challenges were decided.

In the remarkable situation that followed, it was decided that if AAA defeated Queens, the Cup would remain in the AHA and therefore go to Victorias, but if Queens unseated AAA, the trophy would leave the AHA, and move down the road to Kingston, Ontario.

The Queens side came to Montreal to face the AAA eager to show how the game was played in southeastern Ontario. Though they may have been something to behold among the college boys back home, they proved no match for the men of Montreal. With goals by the Stanley Cup's first 'ringer,' Clarence McKerrow (who did not play for AAA in the regular season), and Haviland Routh, Montreal disposed of the stripe-shirted collegians 5-1. Therefore the Cup remained in the AHA, and was awarded to the league-leading Vics.

ABOVE: *This group of college boys from Queens University of Kingston, Ontario was no match for the Montreal AAA.*

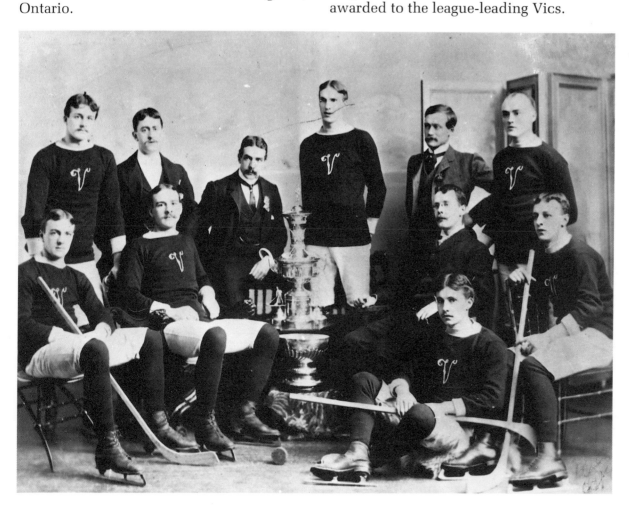

LEFT: *The Montreal Vics never played the game for which they were awarded the Stanley Cup.*

1896

RIGHT: *The Winnipeg Vics wore Manitoba's provincial symbol, the bison, on their jerseys. Note the pads worn by goaltender George Merritt. He is said to have been the first to wear cricket pads in a Stanley Cup match.*

FEBRUARY

Winnipeg Victorias (MHL)

In 1895, the challenge rules of the Cup had been put to the test, and this code would govern play for the next 21 years. The Victorias of Montreal did not get the opportunity to properly defend their prize in 1895, but the Trustees gave them that chance the next year. In fact, Sweetland and Ross did not even allow the titlists to finish the AHA season before sending them into the fray to defend against their western namesakes from Winnipeg, Manitoba.

The perennial powerhouse of the Manitoba Hockey League, the Winnipeg Victorias were a tough lot, seasoned by some of the coldest weather in the civilised world, but they were warmed up by their successful tour of eastern Canada the previous year. They had outscored their eastern rivals (Ottawa, Quebec, Montreal and Toronto) 33 goals to 12, and lost only to Quebec. They had proven themselves worthy to the Trustees, and returned to the East to concretise their reputation as a major force in Canadian sporting circles.

The Montreal ice was ablaze with the scarlet jerseys of the western Victorias. Led by the goal-scoring of Dan Bain and C. J. Campbell, they defrocked their eastern rivals 2-0 and took up the mantle of Stanley Cup Champions.

Montreal was agog at the sight of their Stanley Cup heading west. No sooner had the Cup arrived in Winnipeg than the gauntlet was dropped, and the Winnipegers were ordered to defend against the AHA champs – the Montreal Victorias.

DECEMBER

Montreal Victorias (AHA)

The classic rematch was scheduled for December, and seats in the Winnipeg rink were scalped for the unheard-of price of $12 apiece. Meanwhile, in Montreal, crowds gathered in the streets adjacent to the telegraph office where immediate reports of the game would be announced, setting up what was probably the first play-by-play commentary in the history of sport.

The Winnipegers jumped out to an early 3-0 lead, prompting dismay in the streets of Montreal. The day, however, belonged to the Victorias of Montreal. Led by Ernie McLea's hat trick (the first in Stanley Cup play) they overcame the deficit to squeeze out a hard-fought 6-5 victory, restoring the Cup to its native home in eastern Canada.

1897

Montreal Victorias (AHA)

The Montreal Victorias easily defended their AHA title, losing only one of their scheduled games. The Winnipeg Victorias were back west licking their wounds, so the only challenge this year came from the champions of the newly-formed Central Canada Hockey Association, the Ottawa Capitals.

For the first time, the challenge series was to be a best-of-three affair, owing to the rapidly growing box office returns amassed during Stanley Cup play. The Capitals journeyed to Montreal to attempt to wrestle loose Montreal's grip on the silverware. They might as well have saved the price of the train tickets, as Montreal dispensed with the obviously weak Ottawa side 15-2 in the opening game. The Cup Trustees, dismayed by the imbalance of the competition, cancelled the remaining games and awarded the series to the stalwart Montreal Victorias.

ABOVE: *Graham Drinkwater.*

1898

Montreal Victorias (AHA)

The Montreal Victorias continued their dominance of the Montreal hockey community with a near perfect year: No team could beat them, or even tie them. With an average six goals per game, and 48 goals scored in the eight-game schedule, it was inevitable that they would maintain their grip on the Stanley Cup.

Organised hockey was prevalent in most parts of Canada and in the northeastern United States. Leagues were active in Ontario, New Brunswick, Nova Scotia, the prairie provinces, Michigan, the eastern seaboard, and in New York City. In all of these places, and as far away as France, ice hockey was being played by the 'Montreal Rules.' The fledgling game was rapidly developing into a sport of some significance. Canadian teams were touring the United States, satisfying both their pocketbooks and their competitive drive. Hockey was being watched by vast numbers of people, and although the players remained amateurs, clubs could amass considerable amounts of money by staging exhibition games before the growing crowds.

Still, the mecca of ice hockey was Montreal, and nowhere was there a team with both the money and the confidence required to offer a serious challenge to the Montreal Victorias. They remained champions of the Cup by virtue of their dominance of the Amateur Hockey Association.

ABOVE: *The Montreal Victorias boasted Mike Grant, probably the first rushing defenceman (back row, second from left).*

LEFT: *The Olympic Club of San Francisco practiced in California's Yosemite Park. Ice hockey, played by the 'Montreal Rules,' was becoming increasingly popular across the United States.*

1899

FEBRUARY

Montreal Victorias (CAHL)

The Montreal Victorias' dynasty was to have just one more moment of glory. They would battle for the league title and fight a determined western challenger before passing the Cup to another Montreal team.

In February, the Winnipeg Victorias once again came to Montreal in a quest for Stanley Cup silver. The two teams, having something of a rivalry going, would play their two-game total-goals series before record crowds. In the first game of the series, the Winnipegers held a one-goal lead with one minute to play, when the explosive Montreal offense erupted for two quick goals, the second scored on a rink-long dash by defenceman Graham Drinkwater. The overflow crowd poured onto Ste-Catherine Street in anticipation of the second and final contest of the series.

The game of 18 February was one of the stormiest contests, and one of the oddest, in Stanley Cup history. The Forum ticket office sold nearly twice as many tickets as it had seats, creating an electrifying atmosphere which would flare in the dying moments of the game. The Montreal side defended a 3-2 lead with just three minutes to play when Tony Gingras, the nimble Winnipeg rover, slipped by Montreal defenceman Bob McDougall. McDougall was not to be bound to the niceties of the rulebook, and brought Gingras to the ice with a well-placed slash to the back of the leg. Referee J. A. Findlay handed the hometown boy a bare two minutes for the infraction, which so incensed Winnipeg captain Dan Bain that he took his team to the dressing room and refused to continue play. Findlay packed up his rulebook and headed home, insulted that his impartiality had been seriously questioned. In hot pursuit by dogsled, coaches Barlow and Wilson persuaded the

1899

slighted referee to return to the scene. The Winnipeg captain still refused to continue the contest, and the referee had no choice but to award the game, and consequently the Cup, to the Montreal Victorias.

The Victorias played the balance of the Canadian Amateur Hockey League schedule as Stanley Cup Champions and, bolstered by their defeat of the Winnipegers, fought a fierce battle for league dominance. In their final meeting of the year, the two Montreal teams were tied for first place, but on 1 March the Montreal Shamrocks upset the dynasty in a 1-0 match before 8000 people.

— MARCH —

Montreal Shamrocks (CAHL)

The Montreal Shamrocks had celebrated and boasted their 'world dominance' of ice hockey for less than two weeks before the first pretenders issued challenge. On 14 March they were to face Queens University in a one-game winner-take-all showdown to be held on Montreal's home ice.

The Queens team, defeated four years previously, was ready for another shot at the big hockey prize. They were spirited, but spirit alone doesn't win hockey games. The boys from Queens were no match for the Irish, who dispensed with them 6 goals to 2.

Harry Trihey was the captain of the Fight-ing Irish, and although he was not a Montrealer by birth, he had played a high level of hockey since his youth in Berlin, Ontario. His teams had consistently done well, and he had once been banned by amateur authorities for accepting financial reward for leading a team to victory. His skill was complemented by two other men who would find their way into the Hall of Fame: Fred Scanlon and Art Farrell.

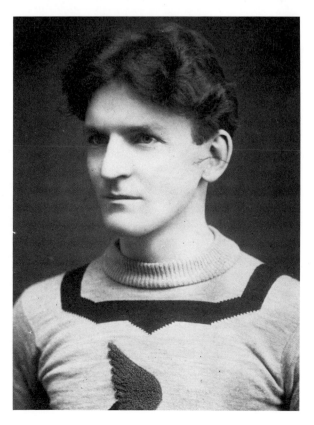

LEFT: *Harry Trihey, the captain of the Fighting Irish, scored 10 goals in an 1899 game.*

1900

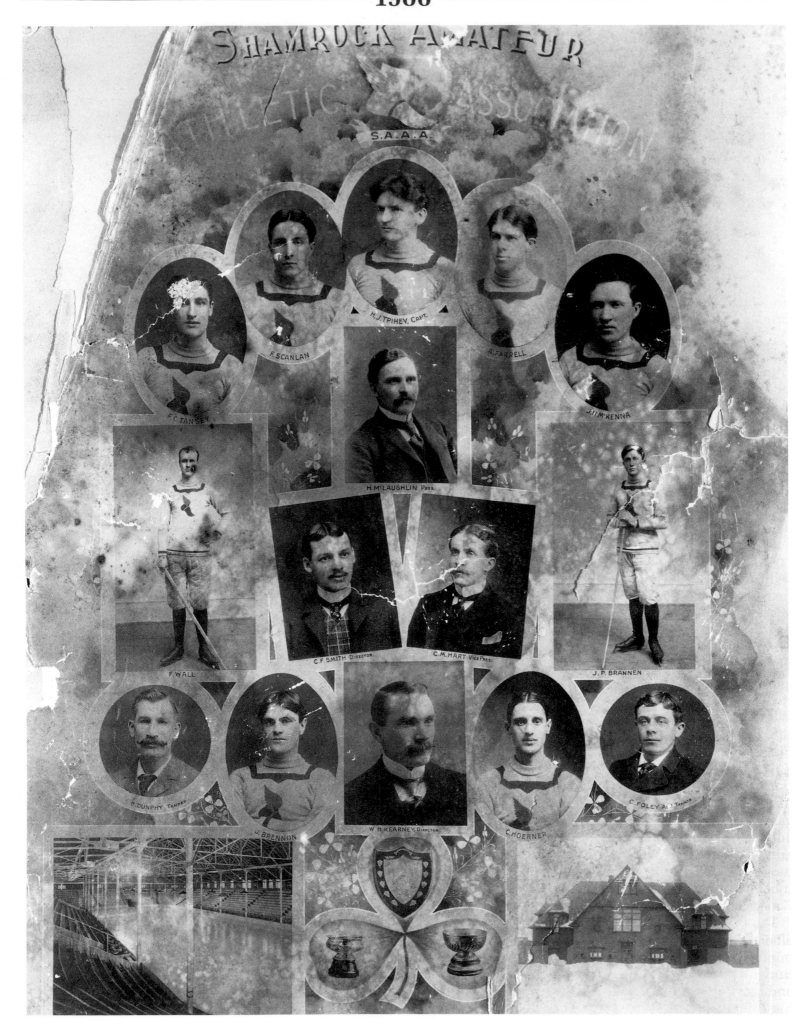

FEBRUARY

Montreal Shamrocks (CAHL)

The Shamrocks easily defended their CAHL title, and with it the right to defend the Stanley Cup. The first such challenge came from those western diehards, the Winnipeg Vics, who journeyed to Montreal to play a best-of-three series against the Irish. The Winnipegers were an innovative lot, credited with both the use of cricket pads in the goal crease in 1896, and with the use of tapered hockey sticks in this series. They used these innovations to their advantage, defeating the defending champs 4-3 in the first game, and forcing the Shamrocks into a come-from-behind situation for the duration of the series. In the first series required to go the three games, Harry Trihey led his team by scoring 7 of the 10 goals, including winners in games two and three. The games were all very close, each decided by one goal, but the Shamrocks sent the Winnipeg-ers home empty-handed, and more determined than ever to return and claim the Silver Bowl for the West.

MARCH

Montreal Shamrocks (CAHL)

For the first time, a challenge from the East Coast was accepted, and Montreal welcomed the Halifax Crescents to the center of the hockey empire. Although the Shamrocks were hospitable hosts off the ice, they were merciless competitors in the rink. The Crescents were something of a force back east, but were seriously out of their depth in Montreal.

The first game saw Art Farrell set a new Stanley Cup record by scoring four goals, a feat he repeated in the second game of the contest. The Nova Scotians lost the first game 10-2, and the second 11-0, and returned to their home by the sea, never to be heard from again.

OPPOSITE: *A poster advertising the Shamrock Amateur Athletic Association.*

Winnipeg Victorias (MHL)

Like a bad penny, the Winnipegers kept coming back. Still under the tutelage of Dan Bain, the determined westerners returned for their fourth spin at the Stanley Cup wheel. Bain was the wealthy son of dry goods merchants in Winnipeg, and was an all-around sportsman and avid photographer. He sported tremendous good looks, a gentlemanly attitude, and a fierce competitive spirit. He had reshaped his team for this contest, and entered the fray confident that he could unseat Harry Trihey and his Fighting Irish.

The Shamrocks had a winning combination: skill and well-ordered tactics. Hockey for these men was not the grunt and shoot game so often seen on the ice, but a rigorous adherence to strategy and proven maneuvers. The Winnipegers, always ready with a new idea, glided into battle wearing new tube skates, never before seen in eastern Canadian hockey matches.

The first match was a closely contested affair, with Winnipeg scoring in the final minute to earn a hard-fought 4-3 victory. Burke Wood split the Shamrocks' defence and came up with the winning goal, to put his team ahead in the series. The second

game is important to Cup lore for two reasons: It was the first overtime match, and the first six-a-side game in a Cup final. Before 4000 ticket holders, the teams were tied at ones at the conclusion of regular time. The overtime was only four minutes old when Dan Bain concluded the affair with a marker that brought the house down, and glory back to Winnipeg.

ABOVE: *Winnipeg captain Dan Bain (back row, center) was an all-season athlete, and a big fan of photography. Here is his Winnipeg Gymnastics Club in 1890.*

1902

ABOVE: *The 'Winged Wheels' of old, the Montreal AAA, were a powerhouse squad in the early days of Cup play.*

RIGHT: *One of the 'Little Men of Iron,' Dickie Boon began his career with the Monarchs in 1897. He went on to coach the Montreal Wanderers in their first and only season in the NHL.*

— JANUARY —

Winnipeg Victorias (MHL)

The Winnipeg Victorias continued their dominance of the Manitoba Hockey League, and were called upon in January to defend the Mug against a challenge from the Toronto Wellingtons. With this challenge came the first of many times the citizens of 'Muddy York' would cheer for a Stanley Cup contender.

The Wellingtons were the toast of the Ontario Hockey Association but were no match for the Victorias, who were seasoned Stanley Cup participants. In a series that went two games, the westerners' aggressive style outmuscled the Toronto squad, winning both games by scores of 5-3.

— MARCH —

Montreal AAA (CAHL)

After disposing of Toronto, the Winnipeg side prepared to meet the CAHL champion Montreal AAA in a best-of-three contest to be played on western ice.

With Dan Bain back after an absence from the lineup, Winnipeg was fortified, and held off a stubborn Montreal attack. Tony Gingras recorded the only goal of the first game, putting the westerners ahead in the series. Game two was a walkover for the easterners, who shut out the champions 5-0, setting up a sellout final. In the third game, the defensive skill of Montreal's Dickie Boon and Billy Bellingham frustrated the attempts of Bain, Scanlon and Gingras. It was this defensive gem that earned Montreal its famous nickname 'The Little Men of Iron.' Late in the game, Tony Gingras got on the scoreboard, but it was not enough to keep the AAA from a 2-1 victory, and possession of the Stanley Cup.

1903

LEFT: *The Portage Lakers of the International Pro League never skated for the Stanley Cup, although exhibition matches against Canadian teams proved them to be able challengers on many occasions. This is the US champion 1902-03 squad.*

BELOW: *Though a pensive-looking chap here, Ottawa forward Billy Gilmour was a tough and speedy skater who played on four Ottawa Cup-winning teams.*

FEBRUARY

Montreal AAA (CAHL)

Although the future would see other Winnipeg teams in contention for possession of the Stanley Cup, 1903 would see the last time the persistent Victorias would challenge for the treasured grail of hockey.

Now accustomed to Montreal, the Winnipegers put up a determined fight to reclaim the Cup. After an embarrassing loss of 8-1 in the first game, the Victorias regrouped to give the Montrealers trouble for 27 minutes of overtime in the second game. In Montreal of the 1900s, it was impossible to continue playing into the wee hours of Sunday morning, and the game was called off, to be replayed in its entirety on the following Monday evening. Winnipeg prolonged the series with a 4-2 victory, in which W. Kean racked up a hat trick. The deciding game was easily won by the AAA, and the Stanley Cup would remain in the East until 1907.

7-10 MARCH

Ottawa Silver Seven (CAHL)

The 1903 CAHL season concluded with both the Ottawa Hockey Club and the Mont-

1903

real Victorias deadlocked at six wins apiece. A two-game total-goals playoff was arranged, with the winner to hold both the league championship and the Stanley Cup.

This powerhouse team out of the nation's capital was led to prominence by the infamous Gilmour brothers, Billy, Dave and Suddy, and the diminutive but unstoppable Frank McGee. Game one, played on Montreal ice, resulted in a 1-1 draw, with goals by Strachan and Dave Gilmour. Back home in Ottawa, there were two names on the register: Gilmour and McGee. The three Gilmour brothers combined for five goals and McGee chipped in with a hat trick, as Ottawa whitewashed the Montreal contingent by a score of 8-0.

It was this remarkable theft of the Stanley Cup by the seven-man Ottawa squad that caused this assembly to be branded 'The Silver Seven.'

12-14 MARCH

Ottawa Silver Seven (CAHL)

In a series going two games, another western team challenged for the Cup. Rat Portage, a hub community in northwestern Ontario, had taken the Manitoba and Northwest Senior Hockey League title, and travelled to Ottawa in a bid to become the smallest community ever to win hockey's biggest prize.

Led by Si Griffis and Billy McGimsie, the Rat Portage squad put up a brave fight, but were bested by Ottawa in two games. Once again, the Ottawa goals were all scored by the Gilmour family and Frank McGee. We can only imagine the conditions under which these games were played: The ice was so bad that on one occasion the puck was swallowed by a black hole in the surface, and was never recovered.

1904

JANUARY

Ottawa Silver Seven (CAHL)

In Canada, hockey was still an amateur game, but the growing numbers of spectators proved to be too much for the American entrepreneurial spirit. In the northern mining towns of Michigan, a new phase in the development of the game had begun. Dr. J.L. Gibson, a dentist in Houghton, Michigan, had overseen the institutionalization of a professional league, the International Professional Hockey League. With the temptation of real money to be made, some of the best players on the amateur circuit made their way south to play the game they loved for the money they deserved. The defending Stanley Cup champions lost the services of some very outstanding men, including the Stuart brothers, Hod and Bruce, and one of the three Gilmour brothers.

Although these losses might have weakened the vaunted Ottawa offence, the roster was fortified by some brilliant future Hall of Famers. Harry (Rat) Westwick and Alfie Smith joined Suddy Gilmour and Frank McGee on the four-man forward line, while J.B. Hutton, Harvey Pulford (both Hall of Famers) and Alf Moore made up the rest of the squad.

Midway through the 1904 season, Ottawa was challenged by a Winnipeg team, the Winnipeg Rowing Club. The challengers from Winnipeg came equipped with trouble, in the person of 'Bad' Joe Hall. Hall would go on to be known as one of the meanest men of the ice. In the first game, which Ottawa took 9-1, Hall paved the road to his reputation with a series of cross-checks, butt-ends and stick-swinging incidents in what Winnipeg captain Billy Breen called 'the dirtiest game I have ever played in.' In game two, in the presence of Canada's Governor-General, the boys played a much less raucous match. The Winnipegers took advantage of Ottawa's self-confidence, and with goals by Breen and Hall, skated to a 6-2 victory. In game three, Ottawa gave notice that they would stubbornly hold the silverware, and shut out the Rowers 2-0.

FEBRUARY

Ottawa Silver Seven

Due to a dispute within the CAHL, Ottawa left the league. The new league champions,

the Quebec Hockey Club, petitioned the Trustees to strip Ottawa of the Cup. While the debate raged, Ottawa accepted a challenge from the Ontario Hockey Association champions.

The Toronto Marlboros journeyed to Ottawa for a best-of-three series, and were outclassed by the speedy Silver Seven. After two games Ottawa, led by Frank McGee's eight goals, sent the Marlboros back to their home on the shores of Lake Ontario.

2 MARCH

Ottawa Silver Seven

Meanwhile, the Stanley Cup Trustees maintained, to the chagrin of the Quebecers, that the Silver Seven would hold the Mug until it was taken from them. Ottawa was ordered to defend the Cup for a third time in one year.

The Montreal Wanderers, champions of the new Federal Amateur Hockey League, arrived in Bytown for a two-game total-points series. The first game was played in Ottawa's Aberdeen Pavilion, which was known for its dreadful ice. Eyes were blackened, noses were broken, and all forward players on both sides found the mark in the game which ended tied 5-5, but under dispute. Montreal refused to play overtime due to the poor conditions, the lateness of the hour, and the questionable officiating.

Because of the tie, a new two-game series was proposed, to be played in Ottawa once again. The Wanderers wanted one of the games to be played in Montreal, and when their request was denied, they packed up and went home. Ottawa remained the champions.

9-11 MARCH

Ottawa Silver Seven

For a remarkable fourth time in one year the Ottawa Seven defended their Silver. A challenge was accepted from Brandon, Manitoba. The Brandon team was the champion of the Manitoba and Northwestern League, and had on their roster one of the biggest names the game would ever know. Lester Patrick played point-man for the western team, hinting at the talent he would bring to the game both on and off the ice. The series itself was a lopsided affair, with Ottawa winning handily 6-3 and 9-3.

ABOVE: *Harvey Pulford, defensive star for the Ottawa Silver Seven. Pulford excelled in numerous sports, but is best remembered as the heavyweight boxing champion of eastern Canada, a skill he put to good use when he dropped the gloves and donned the blades.*

ABOVE: *Never one to shy away from the rough stuff, Alf Smith, along with line-mate Frank McGee, was the dominant forward on the powerhouse Ottawa Silver Seven squad of 1904-07. In fact, Smith had retired from hockey, but returned at the age of 30 to help the Bytowners to eight Cup wins.*

1905

Ottawa Silver Seven

RIGHT: *Joe Boyle is one of the most interesting and little-known figures in Canadian history. Though a well-known event in Canadian folklore, his Stanley Cup challenge was only a minor event in the huge life of this hero.*

BELOW: *The Ottawa Silver Seven with the Cup they considered their private property.*

There was to be no rest for the Ottawa Silver Seven. The Silver Bowl, which they felt by now to be their rightful property, was up for grabs once again. In what has come to be one of the greatest and often-told Stanley Cup tales, they accepted a challenge from a rag-tag band of gold diggers from Dawson City, Yukon.

Joe Boyle was a prospector, promoter, glad-hander and dreamer. It was at Boyle's encouragement that this half-baked assembly travelled by dogsled, bicycle, boat and train for nearly 30 days to meet the Ottawa club. Having traversed the 4000 miles, a feat worthy of a medal itself, the infamous Yukon Nuggets met the Ottawa Silver Seven. Confidence in a game of ice hockey is important, but it was not nearly

enough to beat the Silver Seven. After 60 minutes of play, the Nuggets were down seven goals in the series. Buoyed by the fact that they had scored two goals on the champions, Boyle remarked at how well his boys were doing, and took bets on the following game. Three days later, the Klondikers left Dey's Rink despondent. One-eyed Frank McGee scored 14 goals in the final game, a record which still stands, and the tally at the end of the day was 23-2.

Having spent a fortune and finding no Silver, Klondike Joe Boyle turned even this dismal situation to financial advantage. He took the show on the road, and his now-famous band of characters toured Canada in a losing streak of remarkable proportions.

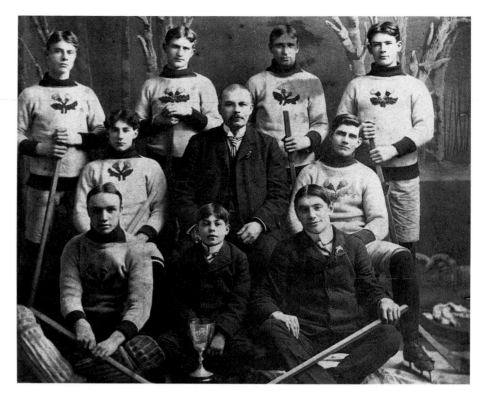

MARCH

Ottawa Silver Seven (FAHL)

The Ottawa club nearly lost the Cup to another challenger out of the 'bush leagues.' A team out of Rat Portage came to Ottawa to try their luck at the Stanley Cup. Rat Portage (now Kenora) was a small town on the Lake of the Woods in the northwestern corner of Ontario, but its hockey team belonged to the Manitoba Senior League.

The Rat Portage Thistles had some surprisingly good players. By this stage of the game, western Canada was home to some of the best in the business. Among these were Tom Phillips, said to be the fastest left winger of his time, and two other Hall of Famers: Si Griffis and Tom Hooper. This talent was responsible for the surprise attack on the Silver Seven that saw Phillips score five goals in helping his squad annihilate the Silvers 9-3.

The Ottawa fans were not pleased with the outcome of this first of three games. It is rumoured that for game two, they salted the ice in order to slow down the game. This would allow the hometown boys to play the muscle and intimidation game for which they were famous. The Ottawa team stole out of the rink with a 4-2 victory, highlighted by Alf Smith's hat trick.

The third game proved to be as exciting as people had hoped it would be. Ottawa held the lead until the third period, and it appeared that they would once again take the Cup home. Tom Phillips broke through the defence to tie the game, with the crowd yelling 'Salt the ice! Flood the ice!'. This only fuelled the fire of fabulous Frank McGee, who pounded the puck home in the dying minutes of this gruelling duel. Rat Portage went home empty-handed, but swore they would have the Bowl at a later date.

The Ottawa squad, after such a close call, took to celebration. A few cold bottles of ale were consumed, which caused the boys to pause on their way home from the festivities and wonder whether they could kick the Cup across the Rideau Canal. They could not. The next day, a weary group made its way to the spot and retrieved the prize, no worse for the wear, from the bottom of the cold canal.

ABOVE: *Captain Tom Phillips (back row, right) brought his Manitoba League team to Cup play on two occasions. In 1903, they nearly upset the Silver Seven.*

LEFT: *One-eyed Frank McGee of the Ottawa Silver Seven set a record with 14 goals in a Stanley Cup final game. His record remains unbroken.*

1906

ABOVE: *Percy LeSueur made the tour of First Division clubs. Here he is seen in his Ottawa cardigan.*

ABOVE RIGHT: *This squad hailed from Queens University in Kingston, Ontario. In 1906 they made a dash for the Cup, but met the free-wheeling Ottawa Silver Seven.*

FEBRUARY

Ottawa Silver Seven (ECAHA)

Ottawa was ordered to play the squad from Queens University at Kingston, Ontario for another defence of the Cup. They felt it below their lofty self-image to wrestle with such obviously weak opponents, and fans felt the same way, as attendance of the two-game series was far below the usual standard. The collegians were no match for Ottawa, and although they knew how to score, it cost them dearly to do so. In two games, both easily won by Ottawa, Kingston scored 14 goals to the Champs' 28.

8 MARCH

Ottawa Silver Seven (ECAHA)

Ottawa was to have no rest, as they reluctantly met the champions of the Federal League, Smiths Falls. Ottawa expected a romp. The Federal League was not as strong as the ECAHA, and although they had been surprised by Rat Portage, Smiths Falls was a known commodity. What they did not know was that The Falls employed the greatest goaltender of the time, the great Percy LeSueur. Time and again LeSueur stood the Silvers' forward skaters on their ears, and although Ottawa eventually won the game 6-5, LeSueur was the star. In the second game, the Ottawa team muscled its way to an 8-2 victory and an unprecedented ninth straight defence of the Cup.

Ottawa may have been a big, mean team, but they were not slow to learn. Two weeks later, Percy LeSueur was the regular goaltender for the Ottawa Silver Seven.

14 MARCH

Montreal Wanderers (ECAHA)

The Wanderers of Montreal tied the Ottawa club for the ECAHA title, and consequently a two-game, total-goals series was arranged to determine both the league championship and possession of the Stanley Cup.

The Wanderers and the Ottawa club were well-matched, but the Montrealers were hungry and determined to eat at the winner's table. And eat they did. With goals by Ernie Russell and Pud Glass, they demolished the Seven 9-1, taking a commanding eight-goal lead in the series. No one would have given Ottawa much chance, despite the fact that the game was played on their home ice. However, the Ottawa squad, bolstered by Percy LeSueur's presence in the net, came out flying and by the third period held a 9-1 lead, tying the series at ten goals apiece. Les Patrick, the Redbands' all-star forward, scored two late goals, and the new Stanley Cup Champions boarded an east-bound train.

Winning the Stanley Cup was easy; finding it was more difficult. After much searching and calling of names, the Cup was found, tarnished from abuse, but still able to fulfill the dreams of sportsmen for many years to come.

1906

DECEMBER

Montreal Wanderers (ECAHA)

The 1906-07 Stanley Cup season may be remembered as the year 'all hell broke loose.' The Eastern Canadian Amateur Hockey Association decided to allow professionals to play on amateur teams, on condition that they publicly disclosed their professionalism. For some time it had been well-known that players' pockets were being lined by the team owners. Now, for the first time, professionals were openly competing for the Stanley Cup.

Prior to the beginning of the season, the Trustees had ordered that the Wanderers would defend against a team from New Glasgow, Nova Scotia. On 27 December the Nova Scotia team skated onto the ice fearing for their lives. Though they were a force back east, here in Montreal, where the game was fast and tough, they were unable to keep up with the professionals. They were defeated in two games, 10-3 and 7-2.

It is difficult to explain the season that followed. In the late twentieth century we often hear complaints about violence on the ice. By this we mean the sweater-pulling, hooking and cross-checking so prevalent in the modern game. By today's standards, what they played in 1907 was not hockey at all. Team owners hired up mercenaries to fight an undeclared war before screaming crowds. Game reports from the ECAHA circuit describe men being carried off the ice covered in blood, players using sticks, axe-style, over the heads of their opponents, and criminal charges were called for and issued around the League on a regular basis.

In the Federal Amateur Hockey League it was worse. There had been a dispute over whether Owen McCourt should be allowed to play for Cornwall, as he was a paid regular with the ECAHA Shamrocks. McCourt should have stayed at home on the 6th of March, for on that day, the hired gun was murdered by his opponents in a donnybrook of epic proportions. There is honour among thieves of all sorts, and at the coroner's hearing the players closed ranks against justice, clearing the accused through witness complicity. No proper trial was ever held, and no one was ever punished for the slaughter of 22-year-old Owen McCourt, who died from a blow to the head.

LEFT: *The Montreal Wanderers of 1907. A year earlier they had unseated a solidly entrenched champion. The red bands across their chests gave this squad its nickname.*

1907

—— JANUARY ——

Kenora Thistles (MNSHA)

The Kenora Thistles, who had challenged as Rat Portage in 1903 and 1905, faced off against the Cup-holding Wanderers in a game that may have seen more talent than any before or since. Of the 15 men who played the game, 11 went on to immortality in the Hockey Hall of Fame.

All the bets were on the Montreal team who, with Riley Hern, Hod Stuart, Les Patrick, Ernie Russell, Pud Glass, Ernie Johnson and Rod Kennedy, were a fast, tough and professional team. Kenora were mostly amateurs, but had imported Art Ross for the contest. Tom Phillips, the Kenora left winger, netted four goals, and Russell scored two for the Wanderers. With only these two scoring, the first game went to the upstarts from northwestern Ontario. Game two is reported as having been a rough and tumble encounter, but when the final whistle was blown, Kenora stood at eight goals to Montreal's six, and the Thistles took the Mug back to the Lake of the Woods.

—— MARCH ——

Montreal Wanderers (ECAHA)

The fighting and vengeful play which had been so evident on the ice was not confined to the rink. There was bickering and protesting over who was a professional, who was a 'ringer,' who would play what game, where, and when, in a relentless flow of registered complaints to league officials and Cup Trustees.

Kenora had buttressed their strength with Harry Westwick and Alf Smith, who had played the season with other clubs. The Wanderers objected, and Trustee William Foran was adamant that the two ringers should not play. He also determined that the games would take place in Winnipeg on 20 and 23 March, but when the ECAHA champs from Montreal arrived to play the first game they found the arena locked, and the Thistles nowhere in sight. The teams worked things out between themselves, ignoring Lord Stanley's representative, and they played the first game on 23 March, with Smith and Westwick in the lineup. Kenora was dispatched 7-2 in the first game, won 6-5 in the second but, as it was a total-goals series, gave up the title and Lord Stanley's tarnished Mug was once again on its way to Montreal.

JANUARY

Montreal Wanderers (ECAHA)

The Ottawa Victorias had been awarded the Federal League Championship, and were accepted as challengers, despite the Wanderers' contention that the Vics were mere bush leaguers, and not up to Stanley Cup standards. Ottawa's on-ice performance in the two-game series did nothing to dispel this view. Ernie Russell's ten goals led the defending champions to a convincing 22-4 decision, sending the Ottawa Victorias into hockey oblivion.

10-12 MARCH

Montreal Wanderers (ECAHA)

For the first time in the history of the game, a team called the Maple Leafs would skate for the Stanley Cup. This was not the famed team from Toronto, however, but another congregation, from Winnipeg, Manitoba. As champs of the Manitoba Senior League, they were accepted as suitable challengers for Lord Stanley's Cup.

In the first game of a high-scoring series, another Cup first was registered. Every skater on the Wanderer's team got on the scoreboard, as they handily trounced the Maple Leaf club 11-5. The second game was not very different, with the Wanderers scoring nine goals and giving up only three, for a series total of 20-8.

14 MARCH

Montreal Wanderers (ECAHA)

Two short days later, the Wanderers were forced to defend against the Toronto franchise of the Ontario Professional Hockey League. This was to be a one-game, winner-take-all match, played in Montreal. The Toronto squad boasted Newsy Lalonde, the very fast and very tough forward of future Montreal Canadiens fame. The game was very evenly played to a 6-4 decision in favor of the champions.

DECEMBER

Montreal Wanderers (ECAHA)

For the first time, a team out of Edmonton, Alberta challenged for the Stanley Cup.

This team had defeated the Manitoba League champions, and thereby earned a kick at the Cup.

The Eskimos were comprised mostly of ringers, specialty players brought in from around the country especially for this series. Among them were Les Patrick, Tom Phillips and Didre Pitre. This amalgamation of stars could not overcome the patented Wanderers' offence, and they found themselves down 7-3 after the first of the two-game total-goals series. The Eskimos further confused things when they replaced two of their imported men with two regular players, who scored five of the Eskimos' seven goals in the second game. It was not quite enough however, for despite winning game two 7-6, they found themselves three goals short of the Stanley Cup.

LEFT: *Bullet Joe Simpson began his career in Edmonton, a city which would wait many years to drink Stanley Cup champagne. Simpson, a Hall of Famer, would play many years of hockey, but never have the pleasure of a Stanley Cup victory.*

*arty Walsh had
Cup play with
ens in 1906, and
ayed in the
International Pro League,
the world's first
professional hockey
league.*

BELOW: *Percy LeSueur
(goaltender) captained
the Ottawa Silver Seven
during their storming of
the hockey world.*

Ottawa Senators (ECAHA)

In the Eastern Canadian Amateur Hockey Association, where the Wanderers played, it was a close season. The Wanderers lost their last game of the year 8-3 to the eventual league champions, the Ottawa Senators. The Senators, previously known as the Silver Seven, were led by the goaltending of Percy LeSueur and the offensive prowess of Marty Walsh, who scored 38 goals in only 12 games. By losing the league title, the Wanderers were forced to hand over the Cup to the Senators. It was late in the year when the ECAHA season ended, and although a challenge was accepted from the Winnipeg Shamrocks, the series was never played, as there was no ice to be had.

| A. J. CURRIE. | S. H. SHORE. | | J. P. DARRAGH. | C. B. STUART. |
| M. J. WALSH. | D. R. RIDPATH. | P. H. LeSUEUR (Capt.) | F. E. LAKE. | A. C. KERR. |

1910

5 JANUARY

Ottawa Senators (NHA)

Late in 1909, a new professional league was formed. There was no end of bickering and backstabbing going on in hockey circles at the time, and although this is not the place for a discussion of the development of organised hockey, suffice it to say that the National Hockey Association was born, amid considerable controversy, at a 'secret meeting' in Montreal. There were numerous teams bidding for franchises in this new league, but there were nine successful applicants. They included the Montreal Wanderers, the Ottawa Senators, the Montreal Shamrocks, and new teams from Renfrew, Cobalt, and Haileybury as well as the Montreal Canadiens.

The Ottawa Senators accepted a challenge from Galt of the Ontario Professional Hockey League, and a two-game, total-goals series was arranged for early January. As had been the case in the past, the OPHL representatives were no match for the classy Senators, and they easily disposed of the pretenders 15 goals to 4.

18 JANUARY

Ottawa Senators (NHA)

The Edmonton Eskimos returned to Ottawa to face the Senators in yet another total-goals series. Although the Eskimos were determined to improve on their previous performance, the improvement was not evident on the scoreboard, as the Senators vetoed the Eskimos' bid to form the new hockey government by a vote of 21-11.

12 MARCH

Montreal Wanderers (NHA)

The newly formed NHA had not even concluded its inaugural season when, with the Montreal Wanderers assured of first place, it was clear that Ottawa could not win the league championship. The Senators were forced to hand over the Cup to the Montreal Wanderers, and the Trustees arranged an immediate challenge for the new champs with Berlin of the OPHL.

At this time, the Stanley Cup was not the only hockey prize. The National Hockey Association was the premier league in the country, and emblematic of the NHA was the O'Brien Cup. This large and ornate piece of sculpture was dedicated to the patriarch of the League, Michael J. O'Brien.

The Montreal Wanderers were to be put to the test against this 'Trolly League' team from Berlin, Ontario in a one-game winner-take-all match. The Germans came to Montreal to try their luck against the Redbands, but with Ernie Russell scoring four goals and Harry Hyland netting a hat trick, the Berliners returned home, victims of a 7-3 defeat.

LEFT: *The O'Brien Trophy did long and varied service to the history of hockey, and today represents one of the finest pieces in the Hockey Hall of Fame collection.*

1911

---------- **13 MARCH** ----------

Ottawa Senators (NHA)

The NHA was largely funded by the O'Brien family, and when their interest faded, four clubs dropped out of the league. It is interesting to note that the franchise which originally wore the banner 'Canadiens' was held in abeyance until the Toronto interests got their team together a couple of years later. The owners of the Canadiens franchise bought the Haileybury club, skated their own, mostly French Canadian, players and distributed the former Haileybury men around the league. The upshot of this complex transaction is that the original Montreal Canadiens franchise eventually became the Toronto Maple Leafs.

The Ottawa Senators easily dominated the much-reduced sophomore league this year, and thereby came back into possession of the Cup.

The Trustees, and hockey fans in general, were beginning to tire of the challenges of unworthy opponents, and for the first time a playoff series was arranged between pretenders to the Cup. The league champions of the OPHL (Galt) played off against the champions of the EPHL (Port Hope). Galt defeated Port Hope in a two-game total-goals series, and went on to meet the Senators on 13 March. This one-game contest featured Marty Walsh, who led the Senators with a hat trick, and the Cup remained in Ottawa after a 7-4 victory.

---------- **16 MARCH** ----------

Ottawa Senators (NHA)

Once again the Trustees determined that the pretenders to the Cup would have to settle amongst themselves who would become the final suiter, and two challengers faced off against each other for the honour. The new Ontario League champions, the Port Arthur Bearcats, defeated the Saskatchewan League team, Prince Albert, and journeyed eastward to face the Senators in a one-game series.

The train fare was wasted on this team out of the northwoods of Ontario, for they fell prey to the scoring talents of Marty Walsh who blasted home ten goals in a ridiculously unbalanced 13-4 outcome.

1912

Quebec Bulldogs (NHA)

The most important development in hockey in 1912 cannot be found in the Stanley Cup summaries of this year. The Patrick brothers, Lester and Frank, had relocated to Vancouver, where their father owned lumber interests. Some called it pure folly when the two brothers convinced their father to sell the business and invest his money in a professional hockey league. Professional hockey was known to be a moneymaker, but on the west coast of Canada, organised hockey had never been seen. The relatively mild climate of the area was suitable for habitation, but it could not support the primary ingredient for hockey: ice. The Patricks not only had to build interest in the new sport, but they also had to build the first Canadian rinks equipped with artificial ice. They brought with them the spirit of pro hockey, knowledge of the game from the player's point of view, and knew who could be bought and at what price. They raided the eastern hockey organisations and bolstered their lineups with the big stars of the day. Newsy Lalonde, Tommy Dunderdale, Tom Phillips and Si Griffis were among the heroes who graced the new Pacific Coast Hockey Association rosters in its inaugural year. They were ready for a Stanley Cup challenge, but ironically, there was no east-

ern ice to be had for the match.

The Cup Trustees made two vital changes to the rules of competition in the East. They adopted six-man hockey, and they determined that all challenges would be played after the regular season was completed.

The Quebec Bulldogs and Ottawa Senators were in a dead heat for the NHA Championship, and in their final meeting Quebec tied the score 5-5 with just 20 seconds left in regulation time, and won it on Joe Malone's dramatic goal, 24 minutes into overtime.

This victory assured Quebec of the NHA title and possession of the Stanley Cup. They accepted a challenge from the Maritime Pro League champions, the Victorias of Moncton. The Victorias were comprised of players who had skated for Galt the previous year. They were no better as the Moncton Victorias than they had been as Galt, and they were dismissed in two uneven games 9-3 and 8-0.

ABOVE: *The Moncton Victorias challenged for the Cup in 1912. The Quebec Bulldogs easily defeated this squad from New Brunswick.*

LEFT: *Frank Patrick introduced numerous innovations to the game, including the calculation of assists, numbered jerseys, and the penalty shot.*

1913

Quebec Bulldogs (NHA)

RIGHT: *Joe Malone, the 'Phantom,' still has his name in the record book for scoring seven goals in a game in 1920.*

Quebec easily defended their NHA title, winning 16 in their 20-game season. The Bulldogs were led by the scoring of Joe Malone, the goaltending of Paddy Moran, and the intimidation of the famous Joe Hall–Harry Mummery defensive wall. Malone scored 43 goals in 20 games, a record which only he could break in 1917, and which was not bested until Maurice Richard scored 50 in 1945.

The Pacific Coast Hockey Associaton did not send a champion to the East, although the idea was the subject of hot debate and testy telegrams. The other extreme of the country did send a suiter, as the Sydney Mines club, champions of the Maritime Pro League, came to Quebec City to do what they did best: dig for Silver. The Sydney team had never seen anything like bad Joe Hall, and though they had heard about Joe Malone, they were unprepared for his nine-goal scoring streak, as they lost the first game 14-3. The Maritime contingent was so weak that Rusty Crawford and Joe Malone felt they were not needed, and left the mere formality of the second game to Joe Hall (who scored a hat trick) and their regular substitutes. The Bulldogs took the second game handily, 6-2, and once more reigned as Stanley Cup Champions.

BELOW: *The Quebec Bulldogs were Stanley Cup winners in 1912 and 1913. Following this fling in the spotlight, they went on to hockey oblivion.*

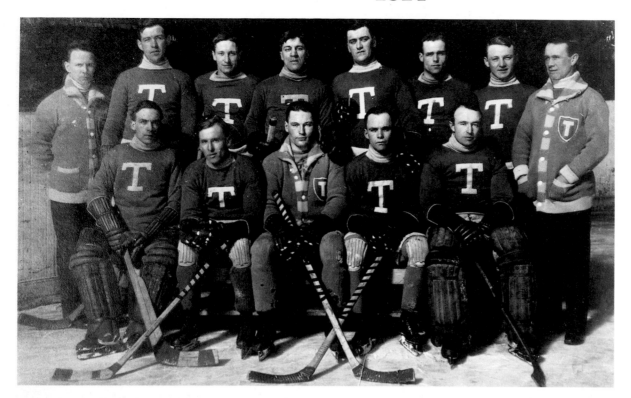

11 MARCH

Toronto Blueshirts (NHA)

The NHA, now with two teams representing Toronto (the Blueshirts and the Ontarios), ended their season with a dead heat tie between the Montreal Canadiens and the Blueshirts. A two-game, total-goals series was arranged to determine both the NHA title holders and the Stanley Cup Champions. The first game took place in Montreal on 7 March under conditions which made stick-handling virtually impossible. This undoubtedly led to the donnybrook which passed for hockey. What hockey was played, however, resulted in the Montreal Canadiens whitewashing the Blueshirts 2-0. The Blueshirts, now on home ice, returned the favour, downing the Flying Frenchmen 6-0 in the first Stanley Cup match played on artificial ice. The Blueshirts thereby became the first Toronto team to bring the Stanley Cup to Hogtown.

14 MARCH

Toronto Blueshirts (NHA)

The Victoria Cougars, champions of the Pacific Coast League, assumed that as champions they had the right to play for the Stanley Cup. On the strength of this assumption, they boarded a train and arrived in Toronto ready to play the Bueshirts for the big prize.

The owners of the Toronto club, eager to hear their cash registers ring, accepted the challenge and, without bothering to notify the Cup Trustees, arranged a best-of-five series with the upstart westerners.

In the West, seven-man hockey was still the rule, and this caused problems for the organisation of the series. It was decided that they would alternate between eastern and western rules. This unsanctioned competition got under way on 14 March, and under eastern rules the Blueshirts defeated the Cougars 5-2. The second game, played under western rules, was a much closer match. Lester Patrick scored two goals for the Cougars, while Frank Foyston replied with a pair for the 'Shirts. At full time, the score was tied 5-5, and remained at fives until Roy McGiffin broke through the stubborn Victoria defence at 15 minutes in the overtime period. With this commanding two-game lead, Toronto started the third game with confidence. Much to the chagrin of the owners, who had hoped for a prolonged series with big box office returns, the Blueshirts, led by Frank Foyston's timely marker, wrapped up the series with a 2-1 victory.

One can only speculate over the possible ramifications of this unsanctioned series had the westerners been victorious. It was only after the Blueshirts won the series that the Trustees' voice was heard. They sanctioned the challenge, paving the way for the annual East-West matches which would become de rigeur for the next 12 years.

1915

1914 1915

VANCOUVER
HOCKEY TEAM
WORLD'S CHAMPIONS

STANLEY CUP HOLDERS

Vancouver Millionaires (PCHA)

The National Hockey Association season was dominated by two teams, the Montreal Wanderers and the Ottawa Senators. From the first to the last of the season, these teams played in a dead heat, with Ottawa playing a defensive, tactical game and the Wanderers playing showy, high-scoring hockey. At the season's close, they stood at 14 wins and 6 losses each, and a playoff was set up to determine the league champion and eastern defender of the Cup.

In the two-game series, the Ottawa club showed all the scoring prowess. They won the series four goals to one, and boarded a transcontinental train for Vancouver to meet the PCHA champs, the Millionaires.

The Cup Trustees had been convinced that an East-West rivalry for the Bowl was healthy not only for the game, but also for the bank accounts of all concerned. It was determined that this format would become an annual event, alternating between locations. For unknown reasons, the PCHA hosted the first of these confrontations.

The 22nd of March was a red letter day in Vancouver. Never before had there been a Stanley Cup match further west than Winnipeg, and never before did the West have such a chance of obtaining the Mug. The teams were fairly evenly matched, and the rosters read like a who's who in the Hockey Hall of Fame. The two goaltenders, Hugh Lehman for the westerners and Clint Benedict for Ottawa, were masters of their pivotal craft. They faced the likes of Cyclone Taylor, Frank Nighbor, Mickey Mackay and Barney Stanley (Vancouver) and Eddie Gerard, Jack Darragh and Punch Broadbent (Ottawa), all Hall of Fame scorers.

The first game, played under western rules, did not go well for Ottawa. They managed two goals, but were not able to keep up with the net-bending of the challengers, who scored six. Ottawa fared no better under eastern rules, and lost the second game 8-3, with Cyclone Taylor scoring a hat trick. The western fans, who had seen their first hockey only three years previously, went wild when their pros made a clean sweep of the eastern club, winning 12-3, with hat tricks for Mackay, Nighbor and Stanley.

The Patricks and their fledgling league had truly arrived, and it would not be long before these innovators would bring about the most dramatic turn in the trail of the Stanley Cup.

1916

Montreal Canadiens (NHA)

The Cup Trustees found themselves in a pickle. The Stanley Cup had been donated by Lord Stanley as the Dominion Hockey Challenge Cup, to be awarded to the best team in the Dominion of Canada. They were aghast when they found themselves in the position of sanctioning a challenge between the NHA champions, the Canadiens, and a team from outside the Dominion.

The Portland Rosebuds unseated the reigning PCHA and Stanley Cup Champions, the Vancouver Millionaires, and assumed that by doing so, they were entitled to call themselves Stanley Cup Champions. They got hold of the Cup and had their name engraved, for all to see, on the collar of Lord Stanley's Mug.

The games were played on Montreal's home ice, and once again the affair was a best-of-five series. The Rosebuds surprised the Canadiens with an outstanding defensive display, shutting out the hometowners 2-0 in the first encounter. The Canadiens turned the tables on their western visitors in game two. Georges Vezina stopped virtually everything thrown at him, backstopping his team to a hard-fought 2-1 victory. Game three was a more offensive display, with the Canadiens finally getting to show their speed and shooting accuracy. Didre Pitre blasted home three goals as Les Habitants skated to a 6-3 decision. In game four the Rosebuds had their backs against the wall and came out flying, opening up an early 3-0 lead. The Canadiens stormed back and found themselves tied heading into the final frame. The 'Buds were not to be denied, and when the ice was cleared, the Americans had won 6-5, setting up a decisive fifth and final game.

The mammoth crowd that gathered for game five was treated to an exciting fast-paced encounter. The match was tied at ones when Montreal's Goldie Prodgers, who had moved from defence to forward for this match, tallied the winning marker. The Canadiens of Montreal had captured the Cup for the first time, and Portland became the only losing team to have their name forever emblazoned on Stanley's Silver.

OPPOSITE TOP: *Fred 'Cyclone' Taylor is one of the most celebrated men of the ice from these early days. He was a six-time All-Star and scored 16 hat tricks in his 14-year career.*

OPPOSITE BOTTOM: *The Vancouver Millionaires was the first West Coast team to capture the Holy Grail of hockey.*

BELOW: *A poster showing the members of the first Montreal Canadiens team to win the Stanley Cup.*

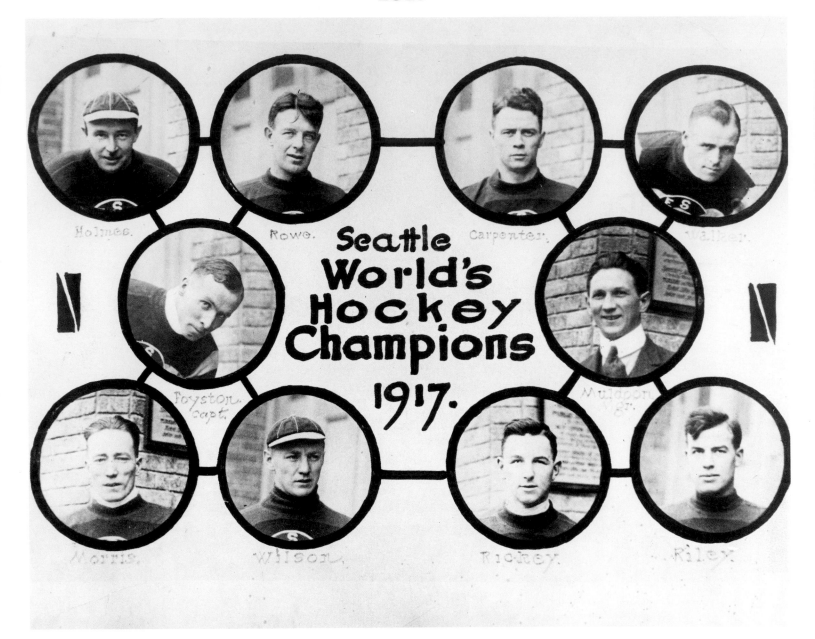

Holmes. Rowe. Seattle World's Hockey Champions 1917. Carpenter. Walker. Foyston. capt. Mulqueen Mgr. Morris. Wilson. Rickey. Riley.

Seattle Metropolitans (PCHA)

This would be a landmark year in the travels of Stanley's Silver Mug. The PCHA had undergone some radical changes, losing teams and finding new host cities. At this time, Vancouver was the only Canadian team left in the circuit, and they found themselves fighting the sophomore Seattle Metropolitans for the league title. Seattle had acquired Frank Foyston, Bernie Morris, Hap Holmes and Jack Walker, and were a force to be reckoned with. They bested the Canucks for the PCHA crown, and prepared to host the NHA champion Montreal Canadiens in the first Stanley Cup competition to be held outside of Canada.

The defending champions surprised the Mets in game one and scored eight goals, half of them by Didre Pitre, while the hometown boys managed only four. If this out-

come worried the Mets, they did not show their concern, and came back in game two to win convincingly 6-1. Frank Foyston was the hero for the home side, bagging a hat trick and impressing all with his bursts of speed and prowess. Foyston passed the hat to teammate Bernie Morris, who donned the three-goal chapeau and led the Seattle squad to a 4-1 victory, and a commanding lead in the series.

The Canadiens were no match for the high-scoring Americans, as Bernie Morris doubled his previous output and scored six of Seattle's nine goals. Only Pitre was able to put the puck past Hap Holmes, and after this decisive 9-1 trouncing, the Canadiens left the United States without their treasure. The Seattle Metropolitans, though they skated an all-Canadian team, became the first foreign champions of the Dominion of Canada.

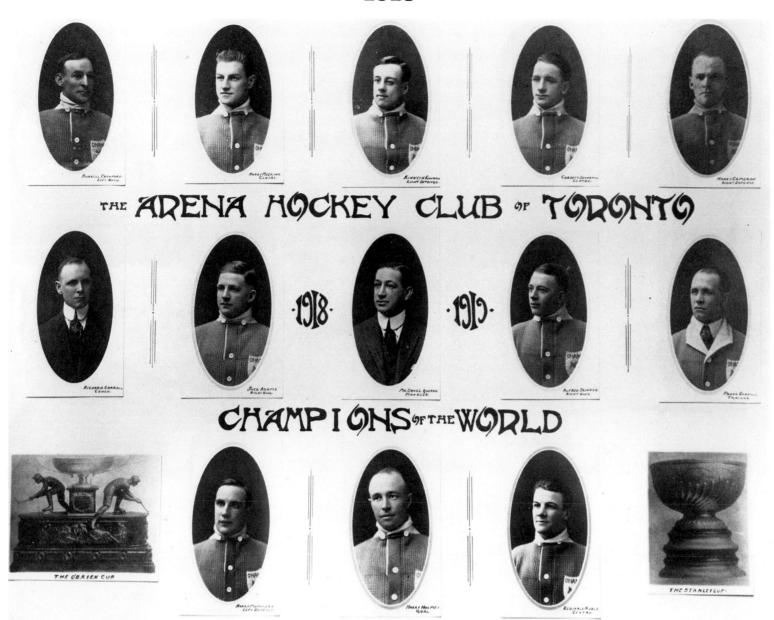

THE ARENA HOCKEY CLUB OF TORONTO

·1918· ·1919·

CHAMPIONS OF THE WORLD

THE O'BRIEN CUP

THE STANLEY CUP.

Toronto Arenas (NHL)

The Stanley Cup had seen a steady succession of leagues and associations, but on 26 November 1917 the future course of the Stanley Cup was paved. On that date, at the Windsor Hotel in Montreal, the hockey world saw the dissolution of the NHA and the birth of the National Hockey League.

The new four-team league assumed the place of the NHA in the annual East-West tournament. This would be the first year that each league would hold playoffs to determine the challengers for the Stanley Cup. In the West, the Vancouver Millionaires met the defending champs from Seattle in a two-game series taken by Vancouver three goals to two. In the East, Toronto played the Canadiens in a similar two-game set. Toronto presided with a 10-7 victory, and prepared to meet the PCHA champions.

The Toronto Arenas came out flying in the first game, and chalked up a 5-3 victory thanks to the two-goal efforts of Reg Noble and Alf Skinner. The second game was more to the Millionaires' liking, and they executed the forward pass to perfection, skating to a 6-4 decision. The gentleman of western hockey, Mickey Mackay, potted three of the goals in his usual sharp-shooting style. In game three the easterners came back with a 6-3 victory, with substitute forward Corbet Denneny scoring two of the Toronto goals. Game four went back to the westerners, who secured an 8-1 victory. The fifth and final game was a defensive battle from the outset, with Arena goalie Hap Holmes holding the Millionaires at bay and the score at 1-1. The winner was scored by Arena substitute Corbet Denneny who, in the dying moments of the game, ensured the Cup's return to its native Canada.

ABOVE: *The Toronto Arenas have the distinction of being the first National Hockey League team to win the Stanley Cup.*

1919

No Decision

The Stanley Cup had withstood a swim in the Rideau Canal and many trips back and forth across the country and into foreign lands, but in 1919 the hockey world succumbed to the frailties of the human condition. In this year there would be no winner.

The PCHA champions, the Seattle Metropolitans, had defeated the Vancouver Millionaires in a two-game series, seven goals to five. The NHL champions, the Montreal Canadiens, defeated the Ottawa Senators in the first best-of-seven series held in Stanley Cup competition.

The Canadiens embarked upon the long, tiring journey west to meet Seattle, hoping to regain the treasure they had left behind on their last western adventure. They would, however, not come home sporting new Stanley Cup jewelry. The Canadiens had to cool their heels in Victoria waiting for the PCHA challenger to be determined, and while there, a number of players developed symptoms of influenza.

Once on the scene in Seattle, five games were played, each team having won twice with one game undecided after 20 minutes of overtime. Before the deciding match was played, it was clear that the Canadiens were unable to continue. They had lost five players to the flu, and although they sug-gested continuing the series using substitutes from the PCHA Victorias, Seattle declined. The Canadiens were completely demoralised when Bad Joe Hall, their fearsome defenceman, died as a result of the flu epidemic that swept the continent.

ABOVE: *Frank Foyston scored 12 goals in the aborted 1919 Stanley Cup final.*

RIGHT: *Joe Hall's death during the 1919 flu epidemic led to the cancellation of the Stanley Cup finals. He was one of the first 'bad boys' of the game.*

1920

Ottawa Senators (NHA)

The series of unfortunate occurrences that plagued the previous Stanley Cup challenge led to what, years later, looks like a bad decision on the part of the Cup Trustees. Montreal had won the NHL season and, as champions of the Cup-holding league, should have been awarded the Cup on that basis. For reasons we can never know, the Trustees decided to leave a blank in the history of hockey's greatest prize.

The Ottawa Senators won both halves of the NHL season, eliminating the need for an eastern series to determine their challenger. In the West, the Seattle Mets again overtook the Vancouver Millionaires in a two-game series seven goals to three, and prepared for their third Cup challenge.

The Metropolitans arrived in Ottawa for their 22 March date with the Senators. The Senators boasted a powerful lineup, including Punch Broadbent, Frank Nighbor, Sprague Cleghorn and Clint Benedict. A crowd of 7500 greeted the NHL champions and spurred them on to a 3-2 victory in the first encounter. Game two gave further proof of the Senators' defensive skill, as they played brilliant 'Kitty-bar-the-door' hockey, shutting down the Mets 3-0. The Metropolitans regrouped for game three, and with Jack Walker's two-goal effort saved their place at the Stanley Cup table with a 3-1 victory.

Ottawa, although one of the coldest inhabited places on earth, was not able to support the ice in March, and the series had to be continued in Toronto, on the artificial ice at Mutual Street Arena. This seemed to give the westerners added confidence, and they skated to a 5-2 win thanks to a total team effort. The clincher, game five, was dominated by Senators star Jack Darragh, who broke through the stubborn Seattle defence to score three goals. The Mets could counter with only one of their own, and at the end of the day, after a 6-1 Ottawa victory, the Stanley Cup returned to its place of birth.

LEFT: *Jack Darragh was an old hand at Stanley Cup play by 1920, and he used his savvy to lead Ottawa to Cup wins in 1920, 1921 and 1923.*

OTTAWA HOCKEY CLUB
CHAMPIONS N.H.L.
AND STANLY CUP HOLDERS, 1920.

H. MERRILL. — S. CLEGHORN. — E.G. GERARD. CAPTAIN — J.G. BOUCHER. — M. BRUCE.
H. BROADBENT. — J.P. DARRAGH. — C. BENEDICT. — J. MACKELL.
C. DENNENY. — F. NIGHBOR.
PITTAWAY PHOTO.
P. GREEN. COACH. — E.P. DEY. PRESIDENT. — T.F. AHEARN. HON. PRES. — T.P. GORMAN. SEC'Y. — F. DOLAN. TRAINER.

Ottawa Senators (NHL)

Ottawa and Toronto were the half-season winners in the NHL, and played off for the right to defend the Cup in a two-game series. The series was completely controlled by Ottawa, who shut out the Hogtown St. Patricks seven goals to none. On the West Coast, the Seattle Mets and Vancouver met once again for what was becoming an annual event. This time, however, Vancouver captured the series easily, 13 goals to 2, and awaited the arrival of the defending Cup champions, the Ottawa Senators.

Game one was played on 21 March before the largest crowd ever to witness a hockey match. Over 11,000 people crammed the Vancouver Arena, and they went home happy, as the Vancouver offence scored three goals to Ottawa's single. Game two was also played in front of a large crowd, although the results were not so much to their liking. Vancouver jumped to an early 2-0 lead, thanks to a pretty goal by Jack Adams, but they were bested in the end by Harry Broadbent, who scored the winning goal in a 4-3 Ottawa come-from-behind win. Ottawa continued winning as game three went to the Senators 3-2, due in no small part to the wizardry of Corbet Denneny, who potted the decider. Vancouver, backs against the wall, tied up the series with a 3-2 squeaker. Alf Skinner was the star of this game, netting two goals, including the winner. The fifth and decisive game was a rough-and-tumble contest, with Ottawa one man short during most of the game. Undaunted by this lack of manpower, Jack Darragh proved more than sufficient for the job, scoring both Ottawa goals in a 2-1 Cup-clinching performance.

With this victory, Ottawa became the first back-to-back winner of the Stanley Cup since the 1912-13 Quebec Bulldogs.

ABOVE: *The Ottawa Senators of 1920 featured no less than 10 future Hall of Fame players and builders, including Jack Darragh and Frank Nighbor, who led their side in scoring during the finals. They went on to Stanley Cup victory again in 1921.*

1922

Toronto St. Patricks (NHL)

Ottawa signed King Clancy and Frank Boucher, and they joined Harry (Punch) Broadbent, Cy Denneny and George Boucher for the 1922 season. The Senators were a very able team which would win 14, lose 8 and draw 2 ties, averaging more than 4 goals per game. Their nemesis this year would be the Toronto St. Pats, who defeated them four times during the regular season. As fate would have it, they met again in the NHL playoffs, with Toronto winning the total-goals series 5-4 to become the eastern representative at the Stanley Cup challenge.

With the organisation of the Western Canada Hockey League, the determination of a western challenger became much more complicated. Now the PCHA champ would play off against the WCHL champ for the right to play for the Cup. The convolutions involved in determining the western contender make interesting reading, but suffice it to say that four series were played, each two games long, and the PCHA champion Vancouver Millionaires were the only team standing when the counting was over.

The Vancouver team played at Toronto, where they would meet a very strong contingent comprised of John Ross Roach, a Hall of Fame goaltender, Bill Stuart, Corbet Denneny, Harry Cameron, Reg Noble and Babe Dye. Game one saw Jack Adams, who had been acquired from Toronto, score a hat trick, leading Vancouver to a 4-3 victory. Toronto took the second game 2-1 in overtime on a goal by Babe Dye. The westerners scored three unrequited goals to shut out the St. Pats in game three, and Toronto responded in kind, winning game four 6-0. The final game was a 5-1 rout for Toronto. Dye scored four goals, for an individual total of 11 goals in the series, and with that victory the Toronto St. Pats became the Stanley Cup winners for 1922.

ABOVE: *King Clancy opened his career with Ottawa but is better remembered as a fixture with the Toronto Maple Leafs for more than 50 years.*

LEFT: *The Toronto St. Pats, with Babe Dye, John Ross Roach and Harry Cameron leading the way, won the Stanley Silver in 1922.*

1923

26 MARCH

Ottawa Senators (NHL)

The National Hockey League season standings for 1923 record a very close three-way race between Ottawa, Montreal and

RIGHT: *Harry 'Punch' Broadbent scored five goals for the Senators in the 1923 finals, including the winning marker in game one.*

BELOW: *George Boucher made history by facing his brother Frank in the 1923 Stanley Cup series.*

Toronto, with Hamilton in the cellar. These three clubs had been fairly equally matched for the past few seasons, and once again, Ottawa played off and defeated the Canadiens for the right to challenge for the Cup.

It was established that both the PCHA and WCHL champions would have the opportunity to challenge for the Cup. Ottawa set out for the West Coast to play the PCHA champion Vancouver Maroons (who had changed their name from Millionaires) in a best-of-five series. For the first time in Stanley Cup competition, brothers would face each other for possession of the prize. Ottawa's Cy Denneny and George Boucher would battle Vancouver's Corbet Denneny and Frank Boucher. The first game was played before more than 9000 fans and remained scoreless until Harry Broadbent gave Ottawa a 1-0 victory with less than five minutes remaining. Ottawa had little time to recover from injuries to Clint Benedict and Eddie Gerard and succumbed to the Maroons 4-1 in game two. Another full house was on hand for game three and Ottawa, forced to play the game with only one substitute available, defeated the Maroons 3-2. The fourth and final game again went to the Senators, with Punch Broadbent scoring a pair and King Clancy getting the clincher in a 5-1 victory.

31 MARCH

Ottawa Senators (NHL)

Though they had successfully regained the Cup, the Ottawa Senators would not be able to sit and gloat over their victory for the summer. Three days later, on 29 March, they were forced to entertain a challenge from the WCHL champions, the Edmonton Eskimos. The Eskimos played the series in Vancouver, as they were assured of good ice and plenty of chairs in the modern Vancouver Arena. The Ottawa side had suffered badly in the previous series, and despite not having had time to lick their wounds still came up with a solid defensive effort. They held the Eskimos at bay in the first game, and at the end of regulation time were tied 1-1. Less than three minutes into overtime, Lionel Hitchman scored for Ottawa, securing a one-game lead in this best-of-three series. Ottawa's defensive superiority shone through in the second game as well, needing only Punch Broadbent's solo goal to clinch the series and the Stanley Cup.

ABOVE: *(Left to right) Lionel Hitchman, Charles 'Doc' Stewart and Sprague Cleghorn in early Boston Bruins uniforms.*

LEFT: *The Ottawa Senators, 1923 Cup winners: (Back row) Day, Benedict, Nighbor, Darragh, Clancy, Gorman, Querrie. (Front row) Broadbent, Boucher, Gerrard, Denneny, Helman.*

1924

ABOVE: *Georges Vezina, the ultimate 'ironman' of the early years, never missed a game in his 15-year career.*

RIGHT: *The Stratford Streak, Howie Morenz, was the pivotal member of the Montreal Canadiens and the 'Babe Ruth' of NHL hockey. Hailed as the greatest superstar of his day, he was named Hockey Player of the Half-Century.*

20 MARCH

Montreal Canadiens (NHL)

The end of the 1924 season brought back the spectre of earlier squabbles between teams, leagues, Trustees and fans. The Montreal Canadiens came out of their second place season finish to beat the Ottawa club who had topped the standings. As winners of the league who held the Cup, they believed that they were in a position to defend it. All comers would have to decide amongst themselves who would challenge. Canadiens owner Leo Dandurand contended that they would not entertain any band of puck-chasers who happened along; the western leagues would have to figure out which team would come east to give its best shot.

PCHA president Frank Patrick may have been a big gambler, but he was a shrewd business tycoon who knew that the way to Dandurand's heart was through the pocketbook. Patrick proposed that Dandurand would pay the expenses of only one western challenger, but that there would be receipts from two series to carve up amongst the shareholders. Here again Patrick had shown his real hockey skills, and both Calgary and Vancouver headed slowly east. They were not in a big hurry to get to Montreal, and played a series along the way, collecting receipts in Vancouver, Calgary and Winnipeg before arriving at the 'World Hockey Court' in Montreal.

Calgary defeated Vancouver in the cross-country series, so it would be Vancouver's lot to be first in line to win the Cup, or to wear down Les Habitants in the trying. But these were the Flying Frenchmen, and neither taking their prize nor wearing them down would be an easy matter. This was the Canadiens team of Georges Vezina, who never missed a game in his career, and of Howie Morenz, who with Aurel Joliat and Billy Boucher on his wings was the star center of the day and the biggest name in hockey. This team also boasted Sprague Cleghorn and Billy Couture, two of the toughest defencemen in the game. This was an all-star team, and it would not be easily vanquished.

The Vancouver contingent played a hard-hitting, chippy game, hoping to slow down the reputed speed demons. They slowed them down somewhat, but Billy Boucher pushed the disk past an ailing Hugh Lehman, and the Canadiens were up by one

game in the best-of-three series. Game two was played two days later, and it belonged to the Boucher brothers. After two scoreless periods Frank Boucher slipped one by Georges Vezina, putting Vancouver ahead. Not to be bested by his sibling, Billy Boucher scored two for the hometown boys, and helped his brother pack for the train.

25 MARCH

Montreal Canadiens (NHL)

The Calgary Tigers were expecting to find a tired champion when they arrived at the rink on 20 March. The Canadiens had fought hard to win the NHL title, and a brief nine days later they entered the fray against the Vancouver Maroons. But the Habs were just getting warmed up.

The winter had softened into early spring, and the natural ice at the Mount Royal Arena was showing the sluggishness of the season. The game was slow and painful for the Tigers. Howie Morenz scored a hat trick, and each of his wingers got on the scoreboard. The game was reported to be interesting from a defensive point of view. Red Dutton clashing with Sprague Cleghorn provided antics that brought the crowd to their feet to get a better view of the shenanigans. Calgary defenceman Herb Gardener scored the only Tigers goal in the slop and slush that passed for ice, and the game ended at Montreal 6, Calgary 1.

Calgary blamed its performance on the conditions of the ice, and insisted that the balance of the series be played on the artificial ice in, of all places, Ottawa. The Flying Frenchmen routed the westerners 3-0 on the Ottawa glass, and returned to Montreal as 'Champions of the World.'

WESTERN CHAMPIONS
1924-25

WORLD CHAMPIONS
1924-25

HARRY MEEKING · HAROLD HART · "HAPPY" HOLMES · CLEM LOUGHLIN CAPT. · FRANK FREDRICKSON · "SLIM" HALDERSON · JOCKO ANDERSON

GORDON FRASER · FRANK FOYSTON · MANAGER LESTER PATRICK · JACK WALKER · WALLY ELMER

VICTORIA COUGARS

W.C.H.L. CUP

STANLEY CUP

ABOVE: *Billy Couture, the capped captain of the Canadiens during the 1925-26 season.*

TOP RIGHT: *Les Patrick assembled this team of winners in Victoria, British Columbia and managed them to the pinnacle of hockey success in 1924-25.*

Victoria Cougars (WCHL)

The wonder of the West, the Pacific Coast Hockey Association, had seen its last season of operation. The Seattle Mets folded, leaving the league with only two teams. Frank Patrick's PCHA had floundered, but he was not to be left on the sidelines of big league hockey. Vancouver and Victoria applied for and were granted membership in the WCHL.

Calgary captured the league title but lost the right to challenge for the Cup to the third place Victoria Cougars. Victoria cooled their heels and waited for the transcontinental train to deliver some eastern talent.

In the NHL, the Montreal Canadiens, also third place finishers, won the right to defend the Bowl. The circumstances which led to this would set a trade unionist's teeth on edge. Hamilton, the long-time doormats of the NHL, had finished first in the league. The players had signed contracts to play 24 games, but the season now included 30 games. The players were not only expected to play the longer season without compensation, but were also called upon to engage in a playoff series. They demanded $200 in back pay to make up for the extra days toiling in the rink. The owners flatly denied the request and faced what was probably the first strike in professional sports. NHL president Frank Calder settled the matter ruthlessly: He passed over Hamilton, and commanded that the second and third place Toronto-Montreal showdown would provide the eastern challenge. Montreal took the series two games to none, and boarded the westbound locomotive.

Montreal would score only eight goals in this best-of-five series, seven of them coming from the Joliat-Morenz-Boucher line. Such meager offensive output is not what it takes to defend a Stanley Cup championship. Victoria displayed a much more balanced attack, and scored 16 goals, spread around the lineup. Four games and nine days later, the Victoria Cougars scratched their names in the Stanley Cup.

Montreal Maroons (NHL)

The NHL sported a whole new look for the 1925-26 season. The Hamilton Tigers had been shipped stateside and re-emerged as the New York Americans. America had rediscovered professional hockey, and the NHL was glad to have the franchise fees from teams in Pittsburgh and Boston.

In the new NHL, the Montreal Maroons had to defeat both Ottawa and the Pittsburgh Pirates before they had satisfied the rights of passage to the Stanley Cup final.

Meanwhile, in western Canada, financial problems plagued the beleaguered WCHL. In a desperate move to salvage big-league hockey in the West, they too opened franchises in the United States, and changed their name to the Western Hockey League.

The third place Victoria Cougars played four games and two opponents before they were given the nod to challenge for hockey supremacy in the defence of the Stanley Cup.

The series was played in the brand new Montreal Forum before huge and enthusiastic crowds. The Maroons were led by veteran Punch Broadbent and a notable supporting cast which included Nels Stewart,

Dunc Munro, Reg Noble and Babe Seibert. Game one was highlighted by an outstanding defensive display by the Maroons, a trend that would continue throughout the series. Clint Benedict was at his acrobatic best, turning back every Cougar blast and backstopping the Maroons to a 3-0 shutout. Game two was a repeat of the first encounter, with Benedict putting on another goaltending clinic. The Maroon backliners proved they could score as well as defend as Nels Stewart, who was filling in on the blueline, scored the decisive tally in the Montrealers' 3-0 victory.

The Victorias finally bested Benedict and the Maroons in the third tilt. Defencemen Harold Halderson and Clem Loughlin both scored to help shut down the explosive Maroons, and the Cougars staved off elimination with a 3-2 decision. The Maroons were not to be denied, however. Clint Benedict proved to be impenetrable again in game four, shutting down the Cougar attack while Nels Stewart excelled once more, beating Victoria netminder Hap Holmes for both Maroon markers in a 2-0 Montreal win.

The Stanley Cup once again resided in the East, where it would remain for more than half a century.

BELOW: *The Montreal Maroons of 1925-26 defeated Victoria to win their first Cup in only their second year of existence. Clint Benedict led the way with three shutouts in the four-game final.*

1927

Ottawa Senators vs Boston

Professional hockey in western Canada had not survived. It was apparent that the National Hockey League had the population base and the opportunities to expand into the larger and richer US markets. Undaunted, the Patrick brothers saw an opportunity to keep their hands in first division hockey, and to make some money. As major movers and shakers in the PCHA and big shareholders in the two remaining teams, they still held the contracts to some very good hockey players. The National Hockey League, in its rapid expansion, would need both players and managerial expertise, and the Patricks sold both to their former eastern rivals. The Victoria Cougars became the Detroit Cougars, Chicago picked up most of the Portland players, Boston bought the contracts of numerous western players, and almost everybody was happy: The players had jobs, the clubs had players, the league had clubs with seasoned players, and the Patricks had money, prestige and open invitations to coach in the NHL.

With no other leagues in competition for the Cup, it should have been easy to determine a new format for the playoffs. But the NHL now had ten teams, two divisions and quite a few fledgling teams which would need healthy box office returns to maintain operations. Two teams in each of the Canadian and American divisions would finish with the regular season schedule, the rest would continue to entertain into the early spring.

In the American Division the New York Rangers finished first, giving them a bye, while Boston played off against Chicago to determine who would face the divisional champs. Boston eliminated the Hawks and met the Rangers for a two-game, total-goals series, which they won three goals to one.

In the Canadian Division Ottawa had concluded the regular season in first place and awaited the playoff between the two Montreal teams, the Canadiens and the Maroons. Montreal took the Maroons two goals to one and faced off against the Senators. The Senators proved their regular season championship was no mere fluke, and took the set five goals to one.

In the finals, Boston gave the Ottawa boys a very hard time. Stanley Cup history was made this year, when four games were needed to decide a best-of-three series. The first game was a remarkable defensive strug-

gle. Nobody scored. Four periods of hockey were played, but try as they might the flawless goaltending of Alex Connell and Hal Winkler gave them both shutouts. In the second game, Ottawa finally got on the scoreboard and defeated the Bruins 3-1. The third game closely resembled game one. After 80 minutes of play the score stood at one goal apiece, and ticket holders went home without having seen a winner. The fourth game may not have been the last in this three-game series, were it not for Cy Denneny's two Ottawa goals that sent the Bruins back to their lair in Beantown to await the 1928 season. Ottawa had won the Stanley Cup for the ninth and last time. To date they stand third on the all-time Stanley Cup dynasty role of honour.

ABOVE: *Alex Connell shut the door on the upstart Boston Bruins as the Senators won the Cup in 1926-27.*

OPPOSITE TOP: *The Ottawa Senators, Stanley Cup Champions in 1927.*

OPPOSITE BOTTOM: *This Chicago Black Hawks team joined the NHL in 1926-27 and featured George Hay, Dick Irvin, Babe Dye, Hugh Lehman, Mickey MacKay and Ken Doraty.*

CY. DENNENY
FRANK FINNIGAN
ALEX. CONNELL
HECTOR KILREA
MILTON HALLIDAY
JOHN J. ADAMS
FRANK M. CLANCY

D. N. GILL
MANAGER & SECY.-TREAS.

The STANLEY CUP
Emblematic of World's Hockey Championship

T. F. AHEARN
PRESIDENT

The O'BRIEN TROPHY
Emblematic of N.H.L. Championship

MAJOR T. W. MacDOWELL, V.C.
VICE PRESIDENT

ED. P. GLEESON
TRAINER

FRANK J. NIGHBOR

REG. J. SMITH

GEO. BOUCHER
CAPTAIN

ED. F. GORMAN

ALEX. SMITH

DONALD HUGHES
ASST. TRAINER

OTTAWA HOCKEY ASSOCIATION 19. .27 CHAMPIONS OF THE WORLD
HOLDERS of STANLEY CUP; O'BRIEN; and PRINCE of WALES TROPHIES.

PRINCE of WALES TROPHY

1928

N.Y. Rangers vs Montreal Maroons

The National Hockey League welcomed the new management of the Toronto franchise. Under the tutelage of Major Conn Smythe, the Toronto club was building an organisation destined to become a long-time force in professional hockey. Smythe had scouted hither and yon to find the best talent available, and in the hunt, found a team called the East Toronto Maple Leafs, and adopted their sobriquet for his own club.

The new names on the Maple Leaf lineup were not enough to put Toronto over the top, and they found themselves out of the divisional playoffs. The Flying Frenchmen, with the line of Morenz, Joliat and Art Gagne leading the league in scoring, finished in first place in the Canadian Division. The previous year's Cup finalists won the American Division race. In Canada, the Maroons defeated Ottawa three goals to one, and went on to defeat the Habs in the semifinal three goals to two.

South of the border, the New York Rangers knocked off the Pittsburgh Pirates and defeated the division-leading Bruins, and went on to play the Maroons in the best-of-five final series.

The Rangers ran into a problem that would haunt them for many of their appearances in the Stanley Cup playoffs. Madison Square Garden had been booked previously for the annual visit of the circus, and the Rangers were forced to play all their home games in the Montreal Forum. Clint Benedict blanked the Rangers 2-0 in game one, thanks to Red Dutton's winning tally. Game two featured one of the most memorable occurrences in Stanley Cup lore. Rangers goalie Lorne Chabot was injured and could not continue, and as teams carried only one goaltender, it was encumbent on 45-year-old manager Lester Patrick to don the pads. He allowed only one goal, and the Rangers won the game in overtime on a goal by Frank Boucher. Game three again featured outstanding netminding from Clint Benedict, who shut off the Rangers attack in a 2-0 Maroons victory. Rangers goalie Chabot was still suffering from his wounds, but Patrick signed another standout netman, Joe Miller, who shut out the Maroons in game four 1-0. The final tilt was highlighted by the finesse of the Cook-Boucher-Cook line, who scored both Ranger goals to defeat the Maroons 2-1, and win the first Stanley Cup for the Broadway Blues.

TOP: *Mayor Walker of New York welcomes the Rangers and the Stanley Cup to Gotham City for the first time in 1928.*

ABOVE: *The three men who brought the Cup to the Big Apple: The famed Cook-Boucher-Cook Line.*

OPPOSITE: *The 'Silver Fox,' Les Patrick, crouches between the pipes at age 45.*

1929

Boston vs N.Y. Rangers

The National Hockey League had changed its playoff format from the exciting and crowd-building Canada-United States showdown to one which made almost no sense at all. The new arrangement saw the first place team in each division play off in the first round, thus eliminating one of the two top teams in the league before the semi-finals had even begun.

The Beantowners captured the Yankee division, while the Montreal Canadiens took the Canuck section. Only one of these champions would go on to play for the Cup. In three straight one-goal decisions, the Bruins capsized the Canadiens, and took a one-way ticket to the final series. Meanwhile, among the lesser lights, the defending Cup champion Rangers mowed through first the New York Americans, then the Toronto Maple Leafs to set up the first all-American Stanley Cup final set.

The Bruins were not only the better team, but they were also a well-rested team. The Bruin defence, led by the incorrigible Eddie Shore and the stalwart Lionel Hitchman, allowed only one Ranger to penetrate the inner sanctum of Tiny Thompson's web. The Rangers played two close games, but were shut out of the winner's circle as Boston swept the series two games straight.

BELOW: *Lionel Hitchman, backliner of the champion Bruins of 1929.*

BELOW: *The Boston Bruins, Stanley Cup Champions in 1929.*

OPPOSITE: *The message on the boards says it all for Boston ice cop Eddie Shore. Opposing forwards beware: Shore deals rough justice to trespassers.*

1930

ABOVE: *It wouldn't be stretching the point to say George Hainsworth led the Habs to the Cup in 1930.*

TOP RIGHT: *Tiny Thompson stood tall for the Bruins, but the Habs cut him down to size in 1930.*

RIGHT: *Dit Clapper, unrivalled leader of the Boston Bruins.*

OPPOSITE: *A one-of-a-kind picture of a one-of-a-kind team, this Bruin squad won the Cup in 1929, but gave it up to the underdog Habs in 1930.*

Montreal vs Boston

The Bruins had lost only five of their 45 games, and were not about to take an early summer holiday. The Beantown boys were organised by Art Ross, who had been around the game since its infancy. He knew who was who and what to look for in a team. Stocked with the talents of oldtimers like

Frank Fredericson, Mickey Mackay and Harry Oliver, he brought up young blood in the persons of Dit Clapper, Cooney Weiland, Marty Barry and Tiny Thompson. This blend of seasoned veterans and hungry upstarts was their ticket to success for years to come.

Again the two first place teams played off, Boston eliminating the mighty Montreal Maroons before the playoffs were in full swing. The second place teams battled in a two-game series, the Canadiens defeating the Black Hawks 3-2. The third place series saw the Rangers over the Senators, setting up the semifinal between the Rangers and the Canadiens. Montreal took the series in two games, and went on to face the powerful Boston Bruins.

The Bruins entered the finals confident that they would defend their Cup. Being confident before a game against the Montreal Canadiens is a bad mistake. They not only ran into a wall by the name of George Hainsworth, but they also encountered Montreal bench strength they had not expected. The Habs took the first game 3-0. The second game moved to the Montreal Forum, home of both the Maroons and Canadiens, so there were a lot of fans standing at the ticket booth. The Frenchmen came out flying, opening up an early 3-0 lead. The Habs led 4-1 heading into the final frame, and despite a last ditch effort by the Beantowners, the Canadiens prevailed 4-3 to take possession of the Stanley Cup for their third time.

1931

Montreal vs Chicago

Pittsburgh would lose its franchise this season, and most of the players relocated to chase pucks for the Philadelphia Quakers. The Quakers would prove to be a one-year wonder, winning only four of their games and finishing so far down in the cellar that they were never heard of again.

Montreal and Boston finished first in their respective divisions, and faced off against each other for a five-game series. The Canadiens prevailed three games to two, winning all their games in overtime. The battle for the finals among the rest of the pack was won by the Chicago Black Hawks.

The Hawks were coached by Dick Irvin Sr., an astute judge of talent. He had Charlie Gardner between the pipes, a goaltender who would finish his brief career with a 1.37 average in playoff competition. Mush March, Taffy Abel, Cy Wentworth, Johnny Gottselig and Doc Romnes were the standout names on the roster, and they finished

ABOVE: *Despite the heroics of Charlie Gardiner, the Black Hawks succumbed to the Canadiens in a thrilling five-game finale.*

RIGHT: *Captain Dick Irvin in full stride for the Hawks, who were slowed down by the Canadiens' express in the 1931 finals.*

the regular season with a 24-17-3 record. They were not a superstar team, but they played solid hockey.

The finals were a best-of-five affair, with the first two games to be played on Chicago ice. Despite 17,000 screaming spectators, the Canadiens prevailed in the opening match, turning back the Hawks with a 2-1 victory. Chicago stormed back in game two, finally defeating the Habs 2-1 after over 80 minutes of action. The teams returned to Montreal, where the Hawks once again outlasted the Habs. The overtime game ended with Cy Wentworth scoring after almost an hour of extra time. The Habs had their backs against the wall in game four and trailed the Hawks 2-1 going into the third period. The Canadiens came out shooting and scored three unanswered goals, two of them by Pit Lepine, forcing a decisive fifth game. There would be no more miracles for the Hawks this year, as the Canadiens clipped their wings in a 2-0 grinder which gave Les Habitants successive Cup wins.

ABOVE: *Pit Lepine scored two decisive goals in leading the Habs to the coveted Cup in the 1931 finals.*

LEFT: *A young Taffy Abel was a sticky presence on the Hawks' blueline.*

1932

RIGHT: *Conn Smythe, the architect of the Toronto Maple Leafs.*

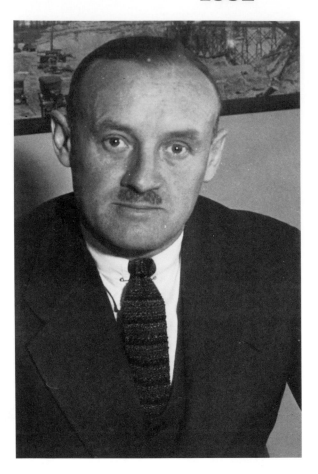

BELOW: *The 'Kid Line' of Conacher, Primeau and Jackson. Conacher led the NHL in goals, Primeau in assists and Jackson in points, as the Leafs won their first Cup in 1932.*

Toronto vs N.Y. Rangers

The city of Toronto was desperate for a winner. For ten years they had wallowed in mediocrity, and as the first NHL franchise to win a Stanley Cup, they were determined to bring the Bowl back to the shores of Lake Ontario. Owner and president Conn Smythe had put all his mental energy, bodily strength and financial resources into the construction of two massive projects. The first was the new Maple Leaf Gardens, which he had engineered and planned to erect in less than a calendar year. The second was the moulding of 16 men into a single-minded hockey machine. The Gardens were ready as planned, though Smythe was forced to lure brickworkers, carpenters and general labourers into the stock market, paying them with shares in lieu of the dollars they so badly needed in those depression days. His team, in training camp, showed all the signs of the cohesiveness needed to achieve greatness.

Smythe spent the unprecedented sum of $35,000 to acquire King Clancy from

1932

Ottawa, adding him to the defensive unit of Hap Day and Red Horner. His carefully scouted protégés, Busher Jackson, Joe Primeau and Charlie Conacher, were on the verge of rocketing to the top of the league-scoring race. All the elements seemed to be in place but, after five games, the team remained winless. Smythe did not sit back and wait for the team to turn around. He brought in the only man he knew could change the fortunes of the boys who played in his brand new Gardens: Dick Irvin.

When Dick Irvin stepped in behind the bench, the team began to win. At the end of the season, they were four points out of first behind the Cup defenders, the Montreal Canadiens. The American Division was captured by the New York Rangers, who blew the first place Canadian Division champs, the Habs, all the way back to Montreal. Toronto defeated Chicago and the Montreal Maroons to arrive at the doorstep of the Stanley Cup finals, where they engaged the homeless New York Rangers.

In the first game of the best-of-five-series, Busher Jackson scored a hat trick, leading the Leafs to a 6-4 victory. Game two, played in Boston due to the circus's annual visit to the Big Apple, was dominated by the masterful defensive play of King Clancy and the scoring wizardry of Charlie Conacher, who each scored twice. The Leafs won the game 6-2 and headed back to Toronto, only one victory away from the ultimate hockey honour. The Leafs burst out of the gates with an early 3-0 lead thanks to two goals by the unheralded Andy Blair. They stymied the Rangers the rest of the night, and finished the series with a 6-4 victory, sparking a celebration still remembered by the oldtimers of Hogtown.

BELOW: *Ranger Hib Milks gets bottled up by Leaf Hap Day in this 6-4 Leaf win in game one of the Cup finals.*

BOTTOM: *A proud Leaf team poses with its first Stanley Cup, in the Gardens in 1932. The Leaf front office included three Hall of Famers: Frank Selke, Conn Smythe and Dick Irvin. Note the size of the Cup, coincidentally growing in size with the popularity of the NHL.*

1933

N.Y. Rangers vs Toronto

A three-horse race was galloping through the American Division. At the wire, Boston and Detroit were tied, with the Bruins getting the pennant, having scored more regular season goals. The Rangers were behind by two games, and entertained the Montreal Canadiens in the quarter-final series. The Toronto Maple Leafs continued their solid play into the 1932 season and took first place in the Canadian Division, leaving the Maroons and Canadiens in second and third place respectively.

The Leafs met the Bruins in what is remembered as one of the most exciting series ever played. Four of the five games went into overtime, and the fifth and deciding game needed an unprecedented six overtime periods before Ken Doraty ended the marathon at two o'clock in the morning.

The Rangers knocked off Detroit and Montreal to set up a rematch with the Leafs in the final series.

Game one was played in New York before a full house. The circus was due again, and New Yorkers knew this would be their only chance to see a Cup final match in Madison Square Garden. The Rangers did not disappoint the throng. They scored a convincing 5-1 win, with Cecil Dillon marking up two for the winners. The series continued in Toronto, where the Rangers once again held the powerful Leaf offense to one goal, and came away with a 3-1 win. Toronto salvaged their pride in game three, 3-2, but lost the decider, with the only goal of the game scored at seven minutes into extra time. The Rangers paraded along Fifth Avenue for the second time, proving New York to be one of the great bastions of professional hockey.

1933

POLICE STOP FIGHT

REFEREE WHO WAS MIXED-UP IN THE TROUBLE

TWO PLAYERS WHO STARTED FIGHT PUT IN PENALTY BOX

DORATY

THOMPSON

JACKSON

LEVINSKY

SMEATON

PRIMEAU

BEATTIE

GRACIE

BLAIR

DAY

COTTON

LAPPER

CLEGHORN

LAMB HORNER

CHABOT

CHAPMAN

SMYTHE

OWEN

CONACHER

JERWA

GALBRAITH

HOCKEY RIOT AT BOSTON — 1933 —

1934

ABOVE: *The Chicago Black Hawks, Stanley Cup Champions for 1934.*

RIGHT: *Mush March, a 17-year NHL man, was not a prolific goal scorer, but on the night of 10 April 1934 he scored one that really counted, in double overtime, to bring the Chalice to Chicago.*

Chicago vs Detroit

Toronto overcame their playoff defeat, finishing first in the Canadian Division, 11 points and 60 goals ahead of their nearest rival. Detroit captured first place in the American Division, followed closely by Chicago and the New York Rangers.

Toronto met Detroit to decide the league championship, but they were unable to overcome the tragic loss of Ace Bailey, who hovered near death as a result of a con-

frontation with the Boston Bruins in December. By the March series Bailey was out of mortal danger, but the emotional strain on his teammates was evident in their play, and the Red Wings took them in the five-game series.

Chicago bested both the Canadiens and Maroons to find themselves in their second Stanley Cup final series in three years. The series opened on Olympia Stadium ice, where Chicago needed two overtime periods and a goal by Paul Thompson to secure a 2-1 victory. The second game was tied at ones heading into the final stanza, when the Hawks swooped in for three goals and a 4-1 victory. The series moved down the road to the Windy City, where Detroit overcame an opening-minute goal by the Hawks to score a trio of last-period goals and take the game 5-2. The fourth game was scoreless through four-and-a-half periods, when Mush March took a pass from Doc Romnes and fired home the clincher, giving the Chicago Black Hawks their first Cup.

BELOW: *Johnny Gottselig and Paul Thompson cool down a hot Chuck Gardiner with a spray of ice. The hockey mastery of these two men brought the Mug to the Windy City in 1934.*

1935

Montreal Maroons vs Toronto

The Toronto Maple Leafs were again the class of the Canadian Division, outscoring their opponents handily and finishing 11 points ahead of their nearest rivals, the Montreal Maroons. The American Division was a much closer fight. The Boston Bruins finished just one point ahead of Chicago and eight ahead of the Rangers, setting up a league championship rematch with Toronto.

Three of the four games were shutouts, the Leafs getting two of these in a three-games-to-one series. The Montreal Maroons took out both the Chicago Black Hawks and the New York Rangers and motored their way into the finals against the Buds from Toronto.

This series marked the first time since 1926 that two Canadian teams met to decide the winner of what was originally the Dominion Hockey Challenge Cup. Game one was played in Toronto, where an extra sweep of

1935

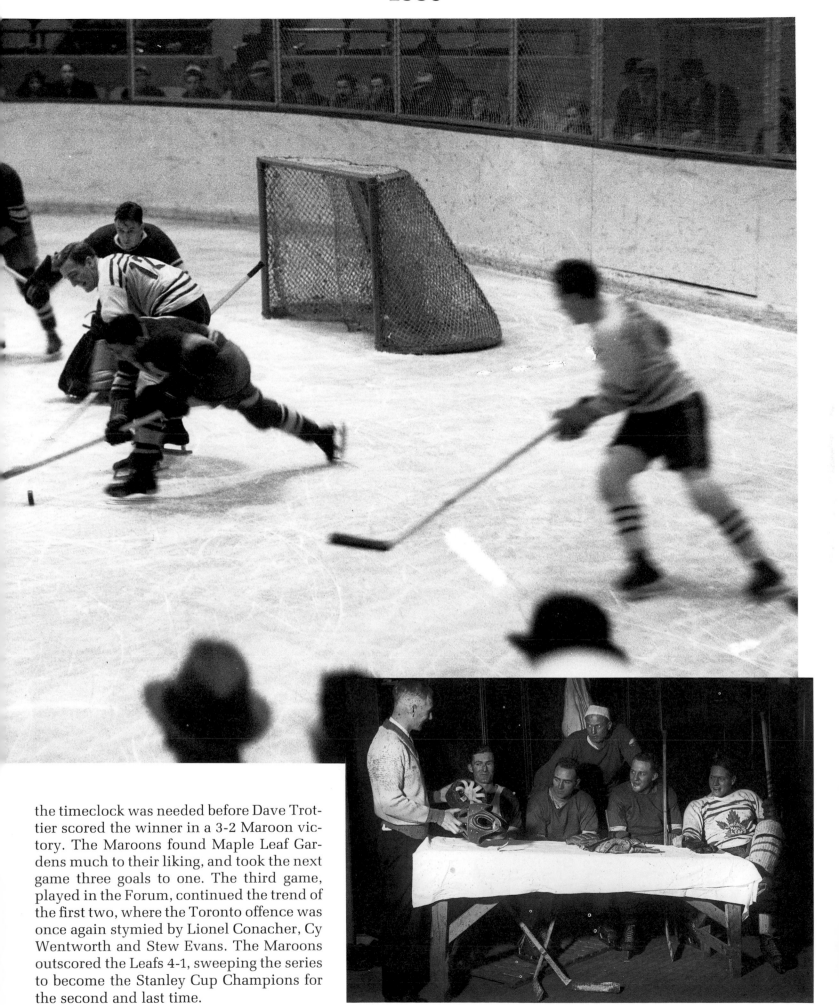

the timeclock was needed before Dave Trottier scored the winner in a 3-2 Maroon victory. The Maroons found Maple Leaf Gardens much to their liking, and took the next game three goals to one. The third game, played in the Forum, continued the trend of the first two, where the Toronto offence was once again stymied by Lionel Conacher, Cy Wentworth and Stew Evans. The Maroons outscored the Leafs 4-1, sweeping the series to become the Stanley Cup Champions for the second and last time.

1936

1936

Detroit vs Toronto

The defending Cup champion Montreal Maroons unseated the Leafs as Canadian Division winners, and played off against their first place counterparts, the Detroit Red Wings. The dogfight in the American Division was not settled until the final days of the season. Although the Rangers ended with 50 points, the same as Boston and Chicago, they were eliminated from post-season play because of their low win total.

Detroit and the Montreal Maroons met in the first round of the playoffs, the first game setting a record which still stands today. It would take 116 minutes of overtime play before this game would be decided by Detroit rookie Mud Bruneteau. This spurred the Wings on, and they swept the series in three games. The Toronto Maple Leafs pushed by the Bruins and the New York Americans and reached the finals for the fourth time in five years.

The series opened in the Olympia, and before the Leafs new what time of day it was, the Wings had wrapped up the game with a three-goal first period. The Leafs slept through game two as well, Detroit bursting out of the gate with three quick goals and cruising to an easy 9-4 win. The series returned to a desolate Toronto only to have Detroit strike hard again in the early stages of the game. Detroit led 3-0 with six minutes to play when the Leafs came into full bloom and scored the needed three goals in the waning seconds of the match. Referee Bill Stewart had barely dropped the overtime puck when Buzz Boll settled the matter, giving Toronto fans something to cheer about. Toronto's sparkle soon wore off, for in the fourth game they were unable to overcome the rapid-fire tactics of Detroit's offensive line of Lewis, Barry and Aurie who brought the series to a finish with two goals in 43 seconds in the second period. Motown had its first close-up view of the Stanley Cup, and coach Jack Adams was to see his name engraved on the Bowl for the third time.

OPPOSITE TOP: *The Detroit Red Wings, 1936.*

OPPOSITE BOTTOM: *The New York Americans vs. the Toronto Maple Leafs in Cup semifinal action.*

RIGHT: *King Clancy, just before hanging up the blades on an illustrious career.*

1937

Detroit vs N.Y. Rangers

Howie Morenz was back in Montreal, where the fans screamed his name at every shift. He was not doing much scoring, but he was the heart of the club. In January the crowds fell silent when they saw the Stratford Streak smash into the end boards, shattering his leg and ending his career. Forty days later the crowds were back. The pride of Montreal was dead at age 35, and virtually the whole population of the city turned out to mourn its fallen hero.

Les Habitants were determined to carry the torch for the spirit of Montreal, and they finished first in the Canadian Division. They went on to meet Detroit, but were defeated in a hard-fought five-game series, the final encounter requiring 51 minutes of overtime.

The third place New York Rangers stormed through first the Maroons and then the Leafs, allowing only one goal in the process. When they met Detroit for their only

home game they were determined to show the hometown fans that their streak had been no mere fluke. As the fans shuffled out of Madison Square Garden, they cursed the circus and could taste a Stanley Cup victory, having seen their team trounce the Red Wings 5-1.

Detroit's regular goalie, Herbie Smith, had never fully recovered from an arm injury, and when the fans crowded into the Olympia for game two they saw a unfamiliar face between the pipes. Replacement Earl Robertson was a minor leaguer with no NHL experience. Jack Adams was a gambler, but a gambler who knew when to bet on a dark horse. They didn't get much darker than Robertson, who was no thoroughbred, but he was hungry for a chance to play big league hockey, and play he did.

In game two, the Detroit forward line burst into action, opening up a quick four-goal lead. They thought they might need it, as they looked over their shoulders and saw

BELOW: *Earl Robertson, seen here in the garb of the New York Americans, never played a regular season game for the Wings, but as a 27-year-old rookie led them to the Stanley Cup in 1937.*

1937

the middle-aged rookie out of nowhere who shuffled nervously in his crease. Robertson allowed only two goals, and the Wings tied up the series with a 4-2 victory. In game three Robertson allowed only one goal, but that was enough for the Rangers to overtake the Wings in the series. Game four was scoreless until, in the game's dying minutes, Marty Barry took a pass from Syd Howe and scored the only goal, giving Robertson his first NHL shutout. Detroit was leading 1-0 in the second period of the decisive fifth game when the Rangers' Alex Shibicky was awarded a penalty shot. Robertson had savoured the taste of victory, and come hell or high water nothing would get past him tonight. Robertson stopped Shibicky and slammed the door in a 3-0 Wings white-wash. The Detroit Red Wings became the first American team to win back-to-back Cups, and their short-lived hero, Earl Robertson, earned his place in the story of the Stanley Cup.

LEFT: Marty Barry was the missing piece in the Stanley Cup puzzle for Detroit in 1937.

BELOW: Les Patrick with Dave Kerr and Neil Colcville after the Rangers' 1-0 victory in game three of the 1937 finals.

1938

RIGHT: *Alfie Moore, a career minor leaguer, stepped out of a Toronto tavern and into the Stanley Cup record book.*

RIGHT: *Goalie Turk Broda played his first Stanley Cup playoff game in 1937. He would go on to play 101 more in his 14-year career with the Leafs.*

Chicago vs Toronto

The Toronto Maple Leafs regained their momentum and vaulted to the top of the Canadian Division standings. The Boston Bruins did likewise in the American Division. In the playoff to determine the league championship, the Leafs, behind the goaltending of Turk Broda, swept the Bears in three games.

The owner of the Chicago Black Hawks, Major Frederick McLaughlin, was a fanatical patriot, and believed that he could build an all-American champion. He stocked his team with as much home-grown talent as could be found in his determined scouting of northern states. He had called up NHL referee and baseball umpire Bill Stewart to coach the squad, and set out on his quest for

CHICAGO 1937-38 Blackhawks

COPYRIGHT
CHICAGO BLACKHAWKS
AND NESTOR JOHNSON
SKATE CO.

Top Row: **Earl Seibert, Trainer Ed. Froelich, Paul Thompson, Pete Palangio, Art. Wiebe, Cully Dahlstrom**
Center Row: **Mike Karakas, Oscar Hansen, Vic Heyliger, Bill Kendall, Alex Levinsky, Doc. Romnes**
Bottom Row: **Marty Burke, Louis Trudell, Glenn Brydson, Manager Bill Stewart, Johnny Gottselig, "Mush" March**

the Stanley Cup. The team seemed to have let the Major down. They finished a full 30 points behind the Bruins and entered the quarter-finals as a very poor bet. To the astonishment of the hockey world, they disposed of the Montreal Canadiens and the New York Americans and found themselves facing the Toronto Maple Leafs for the playoff of their lives.

Already considerable underdogs, the odds were shaved even further when it was discovered that goalie Mike Karakas would be out of the nets for the opening game. The call went out for a goaltender worthy of Stanley Cup play, and in a downtown Toronto tavern, only hours before the game, a minor leaguer by the name of Alfie Moore was coaxed into the fray. Moore was equal to the task and, like Earl Robertson before

him, played and won his first Stanley Cup game. Alfie Moore was ruled ineligible for the balance of the series, and Paul Goodman, a minor leaguer under contract to the Hawks, tended goal in game two. Goodman was not as good as his name would indicate, and he allowed five Toronto goals in a devastating 5-1 loss. The Hawks had Mike Karakas back in goal for game three, and his presence restored what little confidence the club had. He allowed an early first-period goal, but shut the door on the Leafs for the remainder of the game, and the Hawks took a lead in the series with a 2-1 victory. The bookies paid out huge dividends to stalwart Chicago boosters when the Hawks completed their Cinderella season with a 4-1 victory and the proudest Stanley Cup in American history.

ABOVE: *This Chicago Black Hawk team won Stanley Cup silver under the tutelage of Bill Stewart in 1938.*

1939

Boston vs Toronto

The National Hockey League had suffered the loss of three teams over the preceding seasons, and regrouped into a single division. The Maroons, the Ottawa Senators and the Philadelphia Quakers had taken their leave, forcing the league to devise a new playoff formula. Only one club would be left out of the playoffs, and the first and second place teams would play a best-of-seven series, the winner receiving a bye into the final series. The remaining teams would play a best-of-three elimination series to determine the other finalist. From this distance in time, the format begs the question why it required 48 games to eliminate one team.

In the opening series the Boston Bruins faced off against the New York Rangers, who had finished second and 16 points behind the Beantowners. After seven gruelling games, four of which required overtime, the Bruins staggered out on top.

The Toronto Maple Leafs, who had not played .500 hockey in the regular season, defeated both the Detroit and New York Americans clubs to win their place in the ring against the Boston Bruins. The Boston Bruins iced the best amalgamation of puck shooters in their history. They included the

'Kraut Line' of Milt Schmidt, Bobby Bauer and Woody Dumart, the aging and brutish Eddie Shore, veterans Dit Clapper and Cooney Weiland, and their final line of defence, Frank 'Mr. Zero' Brimsek. The Leafs would have to look for a miracle to overcome this swarthy machine.

No miracles would be forthcoming for the Maple Leafs. Boston allowed only six goals in the series and wrapped up their second Stanley Cup in five games.

ABOVE: *Bruin Eddie Shore would win his final Stanley Cup in 1939.*

RIGHT: *Frankie Brimsek, aka 'Mr. Zero,' blanked the Leafs in game four, leading Boston to a five-game victory in the 1939 finals.*

OPPOSITE: *The Boston Bruins, champions of 1938-39.*

1939

1940

ABOVE: *The defence never rests, but Patrick, Coulter, Heller and Pratt of the Rangers take a breather en route to the Cup in 1940.*

N.Y. Rangers vs Toronto

Boston retained their league championship, but the pack was closing in. Only the Montreal Canadiens failed to see postseason action. As the Rangers finished only three points out of first place, it was their lot to take on the Bruins in the first round.

It was a pleasure for the Broadway Blues to take on their New England rivals. With the Patrick family, Lynn, Murray and father Lester very much involved in shooting, checking and managing the New York Rangers, they were a good bet to keep their hats in the Stanley Cup ring. Babe Pratt and Ott Heller held the blueline with Murray Patrick, while Alf Pike, Bryan Hextall, and Mac and Neil Coleville joined Lynn Patrick on the forward lines and Davey Kerr guarded the twine. They met the Bears at

center ice in Madison Square Garden and thrashed them soundly, shutting them out in three of the required four encounters.

The Toronto Maple Leafs swept past the Chicago Black Hawks and the Detroit squad to reach the finals for the seventh time in nine years. The series opened on 2 April in Madison Square Garden, and the Rangers put a quick stop to the Leaf winning streak with an overtime goal and a 2-1 victory. Bryan Hextall singlehandedly gave the Rangers a two-game lead in the series, scoring a goal in each period of a 6-2 game.

The series moved to Toronto for the remaining games, where the Leafs took the next two games, 2-1 and 3-0. Game five spilled into double overtime, and the Rangers moved one step closer to glory when Murray Patrick scored the winner on a pass from Neil Coleville. The Leafs seemed

LEFT: *Action during the 1940 Cup final between the Leafs and Rangers.*

BELOW LEFT: *Bryan Hextall's goal at 2:07 of overtime in game six gave the Cup to the Rangers.*

BELOW: *The New York Rangers of 1939-40, the last Ranger team to win the Cup.*

New York Rangers Professional Hockey Club

LESTER PATRICK   COL. JOHN R. KILPATRICK   STANTON GRIFFIS

FRANK BOUCHER   DAVID KERR   ART COULTER CAPT.   OTT HELLER

ALEX SHIBICKY   MAC COLVILLE   NEIL COLVILLE   PHIL WATSON

Winner of THE STANLEY CUP World's Championship 1939 1940

LYNN PATRICK   CLINT SMITH   MURRAY PATRICK   BABE PRATT

BRYAN HEXTALL   KILBY MACDONALD   DUTCH HILLER   ALF PIKE   HARRY WESTERBY TRAINER

to have game six under control, leading 2-0 well into the third period. Neil Coleville and Alf Pike scored goals less than two minutes apart, sending the game into sudden death overtime. Two minutes later, Bryan Hextall dented both the twine and the hopes of the Toronto faithful, sending Stanley back to Broadway for his last good look at the Big Apple.

1941

Boston vs Detroit

Boston breezed through the regular season campaign, losing only eight games and winning their third successive league title. They were to meet a Toronto side eager to redeem themselves after having come to the brink three successive years and come away each time still thirsty for Stanley Cup champagne. The Bruins assured the Leafs that they would suffer no such misery themselves this year, and fought them to their knees in a seven-game thriller.

The Detroit Red Wings squeezed by the Rangers 2-1, swept past the Chicago Black Hawks, and skated on to Boston Garden ice to face the Bear in his own den. The first game was a seesaw battle, but when Milt Schmidt scored in the second period, the Boston victory was sealed. There was no scoring in the second game until the third period. Mud Bruneteau opened the scoring for Detroit, but Boston responded with a brace of goals only three minutes apart, giving them a commanding two-game lead in the series. The combatants moved on to Detroit, where the Wings hoped the change of scene would change their luck. The Bruins were not to be denied in this playoff year, and they skated to a convincing 4-2 victory in game three and wrapped up the proceedings two days later with a 3-1 win. The taste of victory was bittersweet, however, for Boston would not drink from the Mug for another 29 years.

ABOVE: *The 'Kraut Line' of Bauer, Schmidt and Dumart.*

BELOW: *Led by the 'Krauts,' Boston tossed aside the Leafs in five games to win their third Stanley Cup, in 1941.*

BOSTON BRUINS
WORLDS CHAMPIONS 1940·1

Ralph C. Weiland
Coach

Arthur H. Ross
Vice President and Manager

Weston W. Adams
President

Ralph F. Burkard
Treasurer

Frank J. Ryan
Publicity Director

STANLEY CUP
WON BY
BOSTON BRUINS
1928·9 · 1938·9 · 1940·1

FRONT ROW LEFT TO RIGHT: Bill Cowley, Des Smith, Dit Clapper, Capt., Frank Brimsek, Flash Hollett, John Crawford, Bobby Bauer
BACK ROW LEFT TO RIGHT: Pat McCreary, Herb Cain, Mel Hill, Milt Schmidt, Porky Dumart, Roy Conacher, Terry Reardon, Art Jackson, Eddie Wiseman

NATIONAL HOCKEY LEAGUE CHAMPIONS

PRINCE OF WALES TROPHY
WON BY
BOSTON BRUINS
1917-1928 | 1928 - 1929 | 1929 - 1930
1930 - 1931 | 1932 - 1933 | 1934 - 1935
1937 - 1938 | 1938 - 1939 | 1939 - 1940
1940 - 1941

© FAY FOTO SERVICE *Boston*

Toronto vs Detroit

The New York Rangers went to the top of the standings this season, closely followed by the Leafs and the Bruins. Three of the top four scorers in the league were shooting for the New Yorkers, and they were odds-on favourites to dispose of the Leafs in the opening round. The Leafs had other plans for their postseason activities, and ousted the Rangers in six games.

It was to be the year of the underdog. A lowly Detroit club came from behind, took the Montreal Canadiens and the defending Cup champion Boston Bruins, and went on to the final round with the Toronto Maple Leafs.

The contest opened in Toronto, where the Wings' line of Grosso, Wares and Abel combined for all three goals in a 3-2 Detroit win. This line continued to show off in game two, leading the Wings to a 4-2 victory. The Leafs came out flying in game three, opening up a quick 2-0 lead. Detroit's Eddie Bush solved the problem by setting up four goals and scoring one of his own. Detroit had the champagne on ice, the engraver was waiting in the dressing room, and the Grosse Pointe highbrows came in their party clothes ready for game four and a hot night in Motown.

Detroit held an early two-goal lead in game four, but lost momentary control of the game. In Stanley Cup hockey, momentary control is what it's all about. Before you could say Dom Perignon, the Leafs beat John Mowers twice to tie the match, and gave notice that there was to be no parade in the Motor City tonight, staying alive by a hard-fought 4-3 score. A victorious Toronto team returned home and gave the Red Wings an unexpected thrashing. The Leafs were leading 7-0 after two periods of frenzied bashing and scoring, and wound down the match to a 9-3 victory before a howling mass of Cup-hungry fanatics. After shutting out the Wings 3-0 in game six, the Leafs were back in striking distance of the Stanley Cup. No team had ever rebounded from such a big deficit.

The Wings led 1-0 after two periods of close and careful hockey, when Major Conn Smythe visited his men in their bunker with no certain words of encouragement. Thirteen minutes of regulation time remained in the 1942 season when Sweeny Schriner, with Smythe's orders still ringing above the roar of the crowd, bagged the evener. Two minutes later Pete Langelle scored the winner, and the Leafs skated furiously to a dramatic 3-1 win.

ABOVE: *The Metz Brothers (Don and Nick) join Wally Stanowski (standing) in admiring a tall and lanky Stanley Cup.*

1943

Detroit vs Boston

World War II had taken its toll on the NHL. The New York Americans suspended operations when the Madison Square Garden Corporation declined to renew their lease. The Amerks were to rejoin the League following the war but, as New Yorkers know only too well, the franchise would never be resurrected. This left six teams: the New York Rangers, Detroit Red Wings, Boston Bruins, Chicago Black Hawks, Toronto Maple Leafs and Montreal Canadiens. For the next 25 years, this aggregation would play in what would be known as the 'golden age' of hockey.

At the midway point in the season, the Toronto Maple Leafs appeared to be on their way to a sound conquest of the league, outscoring all other teams by a wide margin. The Red Wings had other plans. Coming up out of a distant third place, they finished the season well above the reach of the Leafs and the Bruins. The playoff format had been altered so that the first place team would play the third place, and second place play the fourth place team. This system would remain in place until the NHL expanded in 1968.

The playoffs got under way with the first place Detroit club meeting the third place Maple Leafs. In a six-game contest, Detroit ousted the defending champions four games to two. The other semifinal saw the second place Bruins face off against the

ABOVE: *With the Bruins for 20 years, Dit Clapper skated into the Hockey Hall of Fame while still an active player.*

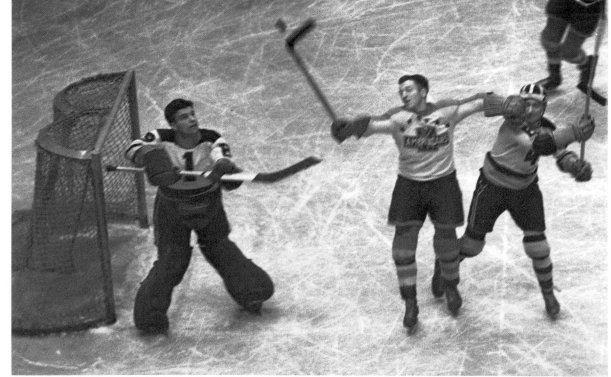

RIGHT: *What goes up must come down, and when it does a young Frank Brimsek is ready for it. Here he is seen in 1939 battling the New York Americans, who would disband in 1942.*

fourth place Canadiens. The Bruins, still led by Frankie Brimsek and Dit Clapper, sent the Montrealers home for an early vacation in five close matches, with three of the Boston wins coming in overtime.

The Bruins and Wings met in Detroit to begin the Stanley Cup final round. Mud Bruneteau took matters into his own hands, firing three goals in a 6-2 Detroit opener. Game two was much closer, and Boston appeared to be headed for a tie series, holding a 2-1 lead going into period three. The Wings roared back with three goals to widen the series gap with a 4-3 win. Hal Jackson's goal for the Bruins late in the third period of game two was the last goal Boston would score this year. Detroit moved into Boston and shut down the Bruin attack, winning game three 4-0 and game four 2-0 to sweep the series, erase the bitter memories of the previous year, and bring the Cup back to the Motor City at last.

1944

ABOVE: *'The Punch Line': (Left to right) Maurice Richard, Elmer Lach, Toe Blake.*

RIGHT: *The Rangers' Bill Moe (21) covers up while Canadiens Maurice Richard (9), Toe Blake (6) and Emile Bouchard dig for a chance at goalie Ken McAuley.*

Montreal vs Chicago

In one of the more dramatic turnarounds in NHL history, the Montreal Canadiens completely dominated the regular season. Coming out of a fourth place finish the previous year, the Canadiens would lose only five games out of 50, ending up a whopping 25 points ahead of their nearest rival.

It was the bad luck of the Maple Leafs to face the mighty Habitants in round one of the Cup playdowns. Toronto surprised Montreal with solid play that kept the games close, but the Frenchmen punc-tuated the series with an astounding 11-0 final whitewashing. In the other round, Chicago took on the Detroit Red Wings. The Hawks had missed the playoffs last year and were not expected to give the Wings much of a battle. However, Chicago jumped out of the gates and thrashed the Wings in a series that saw only five games, and went on to the final round against the Montreal Canadiens.

The finals opened in Chicago, where the Canadiens continued their thrust for the Mug. When the final whistle was blown, the Hawks were down 5-1. They regrouped for game two, but a new force was brewing in professional hockey, and the Hawks were to feel his sting. Maurice Richard scored all three goals for the Habs in a 3-1 decision. Chicago took their first lead in this series in the first period of game three, but Montreal, led by Hector 'Toe' Blake and Phil Watson, erased this lead and went on to a 3-2 victory. The Hawks seemed destined to prolong the series, leading 3-1 after two periods of play in game four. Once again the eyes of the rocket named Richard fired up and he blazed through the Chicago defence twice, and Toe Blake finished them off in overtime.

This win was sweet redemption for Montreal and for their coach, Dick Irvin. The Habs had not won a Cup since 1931, when, ironically, they defeated the Hawks who were then coached by Irvin. After coaching the Leafs to victory in 1932, it took Irvin another seven tries at the Cup before it was his again.

1945

Toronto vs Detroit

This was to be the year of Maurice Richard. Never before had any professional hockey player won the hearts of so many. His glare was the agony of goaltenders and the ecstasy of thousands of female fans. The hockey world was agog at the splendour of his greatest achievement when, on 18 March, he scored his fiftieth goal in as many games.

The Canadiens, led by Richard, Elmer Lach and goaler Bill Durnan again dominated the regular season. It was once again the misfortune of the Maple Leafs to meet the powerful Habs in the first round. After a six-game extravaganza between these traditional rivals, the Leafs stood proudly awaiting the decision of the Boston-Detroit series.

In seven evenly matched contests, Detroit emerged the winner of their encounter with the Bruins, and posed on Olympia Stadium ice beckoning the Leafs to step forward and take their lumps. The Leafs had lost Turk Broda to World War II, and in his place Frank McCool had turned in an adequate but not spectacular regular season. His luck changed in the playoffs, and he performed like a superstar. In the first three games against the Wings, he turned back all comers and shut out the Wings 1-0, 2-0, and 1-0. Detroit came back to take game four 5-3, scoring three unanswered goals in the third period to keep their slim playoff hopes alive. Game five was scoreless until Flash Hollett scored for the Wings and Harry

Lumley shut out the Leafs in a two-goal win.

Game six was scoreless until Mud Bruneteau stole the puck on the blueline and delivered a black surprise to Frank McCool in overtime. The Leafs had come back in 1942 from a three-game deficit, and the Wings stood poised to return the favour. Once again the Motor City was hot for a party when the final game opened in Olympia Stadium. The game was tied at ones late into the third period when Syd Howe of Detroit took a penalty. On the ensuing power play Nick Metz pillowed a pass to Babe Pratt, who drilled the disk past a beleaguered Harry Lumley to once again spoil the fun of the Motown faithful.

ABOVE LEFT: *Harry Lumley led all goalies with a sterling 2.14 GAA in the 1944-45 playoffs.*

ABOVE: *Frank McCool was Mr. Cool as he recorded three consecutive shutouts in leading the Leafs to a seven-game triumph over the Wings.*

BELOW: *A half-dozen happy Habs sing harmoniously after hammering the hapless Leafs 4-1 in a 24 March 1945 semifinal match.*

1946

Montreal vs Boston

The war in Europe was finally over, and the NHL welcomed back their troops. Jobs were plentiful on the street, but at the training camps of the big league teams only the very best of many pretenders would sign NHL contracts.

For the third straight year, the Montreal Canadiens finished at the top of the NHL standings. They were highly favoured to defeat the high-scoring Chicago team, and they did so in spades. In the four-game sweep Montreal scored 26 goals to the Hawks' 7, and comfortably awaited the Detroit-Boston series. Boston had their famed 'Kraut Line' back from the service, and led by this line they dismissed Detroit in five games.

The finals opened in Montreal and, although the Bruins were not expected to give the Habs much of a struggle, they performed bravely in this first encounter. They matched Montreal goal-for-goal in regulation play but could not contain the powerful Maurice Richard, who sent the fans home happy with an overtime thriller after nine minutes. Boston continued their strong play in the second game and again forced the Canadiens into overtime. Though they played hard, luck was not with them. With three minutes remaining in the first overtime period, Montreal's Jimmy Peters shovelled the disk at the net, hitting Bruin defender Terry Reardon and bouncing beyond Frankie Brimsek's reach and into the cage. The Canadiens took a commanding three-game lead in the series in the Boston Garden. Although the score was close, Montreal dominated the play and looked for their names on the Cup after a 4-2 success.

The hungry Bears that were so evident in the first two games reappeared for the fourth game. It was only fitting that the goat of game two, Terry Reardon, would keep the Beantown hopes alive with an overtime goal in a 3-2 game. The Bruins carried the flame into the Forum and looked for the winner that would keep them off the golf course. Although tied at three going into the third period, the Habs turned on the gas and burned up the Bruin defence with a three-goal blasting that forged their monikers into the Stanley Cup.

TOP: *The Rocket's red glare: Maurice Richard.*

LEFT: *Bill Durnan has all his angles covered.*

1947

Toronto vs Montreal

The Habs took the league championship for the fourth straight year and faced Boston in the first round of the playoffs. The Toronto Maple Leafs, who had suffered the acute embarrassment of missing the playoffs the year before, gave notice that they were back on track, outscoring the league with 209 goals in 60 regular season games. It would be their job to take out Detroit, the fourth place finisher.

Both first round contests went five games, and both finished with Canadian teams looking for possession of the Dominion Hockey Challenge Cup. This marked the first time the Leafs and Habs would meet in a Stanley Cup final.

Toronto pulled into Montreal confident they could finish what they had started in the regular season. They had spent most of the season in a bitter race for the league title, only to have the Canadiens finish four points ahead. The Leaf net saw more rubber than a sharp turn on a Montreal highway, and the Leafs were blown out of the Forum with a 6-0 trouncing. They regrouped for game two and played solidly in front of Turk Broda. Montreal superstar Maurice Richard was given a match penalty, and subsequently a one-game suspension, for carving his initials in Bill Ezinicki's forehead. The Leafs, with scoring evenly spread through the lineup, extinguished the fire set in game one, with a 4-0 whitewashing.

ABOVE: *Captain Bill Durnan wards off Gaye Stewart, but four other Leafs beat him in a 4-2 Toronto win, 12 April 1947.*

BELOW: *Wally Stanowski slows down two harrassing Habs as the Leafs change on the fly.*

BELOW RIGHT: *A happy Hap Day and Turk Broda really had something to crow about after the Leafs beat the Canadiens to win the Cup in 1947.*

Les Habitants sorely missed Richard in game three. Again the Leafs' forward lines were productive, and deflated the Canadiens' balloon in a 4-2 contest. Richard was back for game four, but was of little help in the 2-1 overtime Leaf triumph. Richard was not a man to trifle with. When he was hungry he ate goaltenders, and in game five he feasted on Turk Broda. He put Montreal on the board in the first period and put to rest any idea of a Toronto comeback in this game with his second goal, capping off a 3-1 Montreal victory. The teams returned to Toronto for game six. Buddy O'Connor gave the Canadiens an early lead, scoring after only 25 seconds had registered. This was to be Montreal's last goal of the season, as Toronto scored goals in the second and third periods to take the game, set and Cup, and register their fourth Stanley Cup win.

1948

Toronto vs Detroit

The Leafs suffered no second-half letdown this season, leading from wire to wire to capture the league pennant. In a dramatic reversal, it was the Montreal Canadiens who missed out on the playoffs this year, settling into an unaccustomed seat in the cellar with the Chicago Black Hawks.

The semifinal matches were set with Toronto meeting Boston and Detroit taking on the Rangers. The Leafs disposed of the Bruins in five games, while it took the Red Wings six matches to send the Rangers home to Broadway.

For the third time in this decade, the Leafs and Red Wings would meet in a Stanley Cup final. The series opened in Toronto, where after spotting the Wings an early 1-0 lead they stormed back with five goals and held on to take the game and the lead in the series, 5-3. Three days later the rivals chipped away at each other in a penalty-riddled 4-2 Leaf win. Both goaltenders exchanged unpleasantries at the end of the game, and were awarded misconducts for their trouble. Game three moved to Detroit for another round of hacking and bashing. The teams settled down to play Stanley Cup

hockey for the final two periods, Toronto netting the only two markers. They were handing out crying towels at Olympia Stadium in the last period of the fourth game, as the Leafs shattered the Red Wings 7-2 and took the Stanley Cup home for the fifth time.

1949

Toronto knew that to be successful they had to shut down the Production Line. This was their game plan and it worked, keeping these three 'Sons of Henry Ford' from making their mark until late in the series. The war began shortly after the puck was dropped for game one, and the combatants wore a path in the ice from the continual flow of troops marching to and from the sin bin. When the sticks were lowered and the stitches were stitched, the Leafs emerged with a 3-2 overtime victory. The Leafs took no prisoners in game two, spending enough time on the ice and out of the penalty box to score three power play goals and motor back to Toronto with a two-game lead in the series.

The final games did not go beyond regulation time, but the officials were well into overtime filling up the penalty log. These Leafs had no superstars; what they had was the philosophy of Major Conn Smythe: 'If you can't beat 'em in the alley, you can't beat 'em on the ice.' And although these words may not sound sweet, they charmed the Stanley Cup into Maple Leaf Gardens in 1949, and the Toronto Maple Leafs became the first NHL team to win three consecutive Stanley Cups.

BELOW: *Bill Ezinicki bends the hemp, leading the Leafs to a 3-1 victory in game three, 13 April 1949.*

Toronto vs Detroit

Detroit Red Wings' boss Jack Adams had spotted a talented youngster at the New York Rangers training camp a few years back, and had brought him into the fold. This tall, lean fellow from Floral, Saskatchewan had timing, leadership potential and quick elbows. Jack Adams smelled a superstar in Gordie Howe. Howe's first two seasons were unremarkable, but in this, his third, he was shifted onto a line with Ted Lindsay and Sid Abel, and Howe's considerable talents finally began to shine. This 'Production Line' led the Wings to the league pennant, a slot they would not relinquish for another seven years.

Matchups in the semifinals saw the Wings play the Canadiens and the Boston Bruins face the defending Cup champion Maple Leafs, who had come within a whisker of missing the postseason. In a hard seven-game series the Detroit Red Wings snuck past the Habs while the Leafs, always saving their best for last, eliminated the Boston club in just five games.

Once again the Leafs and the Wings would do battle in a Stanley Cup final.

1950

Detroit vs New York

The Detroit goal-scoring factory was up to full production when the decade opened. Lindsay, Abel and Howe finished 1-2-3 in the scoring race, and the Wings finished with a convincing 11-point margin in the league standings. They were to meet their perennial foes, the Toronto Maple Leafs, in the semifinal round. In one of the roughest and bloodiest semis of all time, the Wings staggered out of a thrilling seven-game series to meet the New York Rangers.

The Rangers had eliminated the Montreal Canadiens in five games and reached the finals for the first time since 1937. The first game of the Ranger-Wings contest established that these teams were more interested in playing hockey than in watching it happen from the penalty box. The Wings, on the strength of four second period goals, took game one in convincing fashion, 4-1. Game two saw the Rangers skate back to even the tilt. Edgar Laprade scored two third period goals and the Rangers held on for a 3-1 victory.

The series was to return to New York, but as New Yorkers seemed to be more interested in the circus than in hockey, the Rangers were forced to play all but one game on Red Wings home ice. Game three, played in Toronto, was dominated by Detroit. They shut out the Rangers 4-0 and headed back home knowing that the remaining games would be played for a faithful hometown crowd. The Rangers appeared to be on their way to another loss when Gus Kyle scored with minutes remaining in the third period, sending the game into overtime. Don Raleigh reversed the fortunes of the Blueshirts with a dramatic banger at eight minutes in the overtime session.

Game five was hockey played at its defensive best. The Rangers held a 1-0 lead when, with less than two minutes remaining, Ted Lindsay took a pass from Sid Abel and manufactured the tying goal for the Wings. Don Raleigh had a flair for the dramatic, and he repeated his heroics of game four, scoring at 1:38 of overtime to bring the Rangers within one game of their third Stanley Cup. Game six was played largely in the Detroit end of the rink, but the Wings took flight with two late goals in the third period to defeat the Rangers 5-4 and set up what would become one of the most thrilling games in Stanley Cup history.

When game seven began, the Detroit Red

Wings were back to their old bad habits, and took two unnecessary penalties in the first period, setting up the Rangers for two successful power plays. Detroit stole a page from the Rangers' book and scored two power play goals of their own in the second period, tying the affair. The game stood at 3-3 when the clock ran out. They grappled through the first overtime period, and marched off to the dressing room for 15 minutes of respite. Sudden death hockey brings out strange things in hockey players. So often it is the lesser lights who come to life while the stars rarely shine. The second overtime was eight minutes old when Pete Babando was slipped a pass by George Gee. With a flick of the wrist the red light flashed, and the lights went out for the Rangers. Pete Babando was the toast of Detroit and, for that brief moment in Stanley Cup time, his name was on the lips of hockey fans from coast to coast. The Detroit Red Wings had won their fourth Stanley Cup.

ABOVE: *Pete Babando was a Motown hero after his dramatic goal in double overtime of game seven gave the Wings the Cup, 23 April 1950.*

ABOVE: *Harry Lumley is tested from close range by Don Raleigh in game three, 15 April 1950. Lumley stopped all comers in a 4-0 whitewash.*

LEFT: *Pat Egan (6) and Allan Stanley cover up for Chuck Rayner as Al Dewsbury searches for the rebound.*

1951

Toronto vs Montreal

Detroit continued to dominate the National Hockey League, and this year would face the Montreal Canadiens in the first round of postseason play. The Canadiens had finished third in the league standings, and a full 36 points behind the Wings.

The six-game series was a very polite bit of hockey. Detroit hosted the first pair of games and lost them both, and the Canadiens returned the favour by losing games three and four in Montreal. When the series moved back to Detroit for game five, the Habs continued the pattern, winning a 5-2 rafter-shaker in Olympia Stadium. A deflated squad of league champions returned from game six in Montreal, as the Habitants skated by them 3-2 on goals by Richard, Mosdell and Reay. So calm was this game that no penalties were assessed for either side.

In the other round, Boston took one game from the Leafs, tied one (the Sunday law in Toronto ended the 1-1 match), and lost the next four straight, setting up a classic Montreal-Toronto confrontation.

The series that followed climaxed in an image which is still one of the most requested photographs in the Hall of Fame library. The drama began to unfold as the Leafs wrestled to an overtime win in the first game at Maple Leaf Gardens. In game two the sides exchanged goals during regular time, and the match went into overtime. At 2:55, Maurice Richard took a pass from Doug Harvey and blew the puck past Broda, sending them all off to the Forum for game

three. Again overtime was needed to decide the winner, but Toronto's Teeder Kennedy stopped the clock at 4:47 and put the Leafs ahead in the series. Two days later the Montreal fans watched from the edge of their seats as another Maple Leaf, Harry Watson, stopped the Habs in the first period of overtime, and it was back to Toronto for game five.

Rocket Richard was not prepared to give up the Cup, and scored one of his patented goals, teasing Al Rollins out of his cage and slipping 'le rondelle' into an empty net. The Leafs tied the game moments later, but in the third period Les Habitants went up by one. As the clock ran down, the Leafs regrouped but were unable to find a hole in the defence. With 32 seconds remaining, Al Rollins skated to the bench, and the Leaf

attack squad, six men strong, burst over the blueline, giving Tod Sloan his second tying goal of the night.

For the fifth time in the series they wound up the overtime clock, but before the three-minute mark had been reached, Maple Leaf Gardens exploded. Harry Watson gathered in a rolling puck and shuffled it to Howie Meeker. Meeker took the puck behind the Canadiens' net and made a long pass to defenceman Bill Barilko. Barilko one-timed the disk, and it was over. The Toronto Maple Leafs were Stanley Cup Champions, but Bill Barilko had scored his last goal. Some months later he was lost and presumed dead when his bush plane disappeared in northern Ontario. The Maple Leafs would not win the Cup again until Barilko's body was found, ten years later.

LEFT: *Bill Barilko relaxes after scoring the winning marker in the 1950-51 finals. Barilko would lose his life in a plane crash later that summer, and an era of Leaf dominance would die with him.*

1952

Detroit vs Montreal

For the second time, the Detroit Red Wings gathered 100 points in the regular season. Howe and Lindsay were 1-2 in the scoring race and goaltender Terry Sawchuk won the Vezina Trophy. This was to be the year of the Red Wings. First on the agenda was a series with the defending Cup champion Leafs, whom they disposed of in four games. The Leafs scored a meagre three goals in the entire series and were already calculating their handicaps on the golf course when the Canadiens defeated the Bruins in a seven-game playdown.

The 1952 version of the Stanley Cup finals opened on 10 April in Montreal. It was highlighted by a bizarre occurrence near the end of the game. The Wings held a 2-0 lead thanks to a brace of goals by Tony Leswick. Tom Johnson's tally put the Habs within striking distance of a tie, and when the announcement came that there was one minute remaining, Dick Irvin pulled the goalie. The plan backfired when Detroit won the draw and Ted Lindsay fired the puck into the yawning cage. It was only later that the Habs discovered that the announcer had been wrong. There were two minutes to play, and a frustrated Dick Irvin could, in the end, only shrug and send his boys off to the showers.

Game two was a bitterly fought, low scoring contest. Ted Lindsay scored the winning goal and the Wings returned to Detroit two games up in the series. On home ice the Wings were unstoppable. In game three, Detroit scored in each period and left the rest to Terry Sawchuk, who stopped everything in the 3-0 win. Detroit liked the game plan for game three so well they followed it to the letter in the fourth game. Metro Prystai potted a pair of goals, Terry Sawchuk recorded his fourth shutout in eight playoff games, and the Stanley Cup returned to the banks of the Detroit River.

It is very much worth noting that another team challenged for the Stanley Cup this year. In March 1953, the Cleveland Barons of the American Hockey League sent a proposal to the NHL, requesting a challenge should their club win the AHL title. The NHL, who by then had assumed the rights previously held by the Cup Trustees, declined. They felt that the Barons were swimming in water well over their heads.

BELOW: *The 'Production Line' of (l-r) Howe, Abel and Lindsay. This trio led the Wings to seven consecutive first place finishes from 1948-49 to 1954-55. In 1951-52, Howe and Lindsay finished 1-2 in the scoring race.*

1953

Montreal vs Boston

Detroit's win total was down somewhat this season, but they still appeared to be strong contenders for the Cup. Gordie Howe again won the scoring title, and Terry Sawchuk was the best 'plumber' between the pipes in the NHL. Once again Detroit stood at the top of the league standings, braced to meet the Boston Bruins in the first round.

Boston had finished 21 points behind Detroit and were serious underdogs going into Olympia Stadium. The Bruins rebounded from an opening game thrashing to win four of the next five and send a shell-shocked Detroit team off for their final post-game shower of the season. The other series pitted the Canadiens against the Black Hawks. The teams were evenly matched and they played a seesaw series for seven games, with Montreal taking the final.

The Canadiens prepared to meet Boston in the final round. The team brass were not happy with the goaltending situation and had called up a young rookie to replace Gerry McNeil in the Chicago semifinal series. This rookie was Jacques Plante, and he responded with a shutout in his first NHL playoff game. Coach Irvin decided to go with Plante, and he was guarding the twine when the series opened.

Montreal played a cautious but effective first game and took it 4-2. In game two the Bruins regrouped and solved the Jacques Plante mystery, shoving four pills behind him in a 4-1 Boston victory. By game three the Boston well had run dry. Gerry McNeil was back in the Montreal net, and he backstopped the Montrealers to a 3-0 decision. The Bruins tried to open up game four, hoping somehow to break down the defensive barrier the Habs had set up around their man in the net. The Canadiens scored early and often, sending the Bruins to the brink of elimination with a 7-3 pounding.

Game five was back at the Montreal Forum, where Boston reversed their game plan once again and engaged the Habs in a tough defensive battle. There was no scoring in regulation time and the teams prepared for the first overtime in the series. The crowd had barely made their way back to their seats when Elmer Lach secured a pass from Rocket Richard and fired it past Sugar Jim Henry. Richard, a man with powerful emotions, was so overcome by the sweetness of triumph that his embrace broke the nose of hero Elmer Lach.

ABOVE: *Terry Sawchuk, here with the Omaha Knights of the USHL, couldn't take the Wings back to the finals in 1953.*

BELOW: *The steady defence of Butch Bouchard, Tom Johnson and Jacques Plante brought the Cup to Montreal in 1953.*

1954

Detroit vs Montreal

Detroit won the league title for the sixth consecutive time, although their margin of victory was the slimmest it had been in years. The Toronto Maple Leafs rebounded from a dismal 1953 season and prepared to meet the Wings in the opening round.

It took Detroit only five games to overcome the Leafs in a closely contested series. The Montreal Canadiens had finished a strong second to Detroit and knocked off the Boston Bruins in four straight games, with Jacques Plante recording two shutouts. Montreal travelled to Detroit for a rematch of the 1952 finals.

Game one featured rough play and a number of penalties. Scoring was at a premium until the third period when the Wings scored a power-play marker and a short-handed goal to put the game out of the reach of the Montreal Canadiens. Detroit were two men down in the first period of game two and the Habs made them pay for the manpower shortage. The Montreal special teams scored three goals in 56 seconds and held on for a 3-1 series-tying win. The scene shifted to Montreal for game three. Alex Delvecchio opened the game with a goal at the 42-second mark, putting the Wings ahead to stay.

Detroit took over in game four and shut down the Canadiens in a 2-0 varnishing. Montreal turned the tables on the Wings in game five. Gerry McNeil was back in the net

BELOW: *Why are these men smiling? Geoffrion, Richard and Beliveau had just finished 1-2-3 in the league scoring race.*

for Montreal and repeated his game five shutout feat of the previous season. Les Habitants clung to life again in game six, helped by three quick goals in the second period, two by Floyd Curry, the other by Bernie 'Boom Boom' Geoffrion. Detroit would beat McNeil only once, and the weary pros traipsed back to the Motor City for the final showdown. Montreal jumped on the scoreboard first, Floyd Curry performing the honours. Red Kelly, an offence-minded defenceman, pulled Detroit even on a second period power play. The remainder of the game would be scoreless, setting up only the second seventh-game overtime in Stanley Cup history. Four minutes into extra time, winger Tony Leswick took a pass from Glen Skov, crossed over the blueline and pitched the puck into the fray, hitting Montreal defender Doug Harvey and bouncing past a stunned Gerry McNeil.

Stanley Cup history was made when President Clarence Campbell presented the Mug to the president of the Detroit Red Wings, Miss Marguerite Norris. She remains the only woman to have her name hammered into Stanley Cup silver.

1955

Detroit vs Montreal

For the seventh straight year, the Detroit Red Wings surveyed the lay of the land from their lofty perch atop the NHL standings. Their elevated position was a precarious one this year, as they had to thrash the Canadiens 6-0 in their final regular season game to maintain their consecutive pennant run.

When the great Red Wings met the Toronto Maple Leafs, they were at the peak of their performance. Though the Leafs put up a brave fight, they succumbed to the Wings in four straight.

The Canadiens were to play the Boston Bruins, but they would have to do it without Maurice Richard. Following a brutish attack on Boston defenceman Hal Laycoe in a regular season game on 13 March, Richard took after the linesman called in to restrain him. In what would prove to be the most controversial officiating decision NHL President Clarence Campbell ever made, Richard was barred from further play in the season and in the playoffs. The people of Montreal were outraged by the severity of the suspension, and thousands took out their frustrations on the shopkeepers of downtown Montreal. The ensuing riot came to a conclusion only when Richard himself took to the airwaves in an appeal to his fans to cease and desist.

The Canadiens, despite Rocket Richard's absence, handled the Bruins easily, taking them out in five games. The resulting seven-game series between Detroit and the Montrealers was a bitter struggle, and in retrospect is memorable only for Richard's absence.

Games one and two were dominated by the Wings. Detroit scored the final three goals of game one to win 4-2, and the first seven goals of game two to annihilate the Habs 7-1. Montreal fought back on home ice to take games three and four by scores of 4-2 and 5-3 respectively. The teams split games five and six. Gordie Howe scored a hat trick to lead the Redbirds to a 5-1 victory in the fifth game, and Boom Boom Geoffrion scored a pair to even up the series in a 6-3 Montreal triumph. The seventh game was played in Detroit. The Wings shut down the Beliveau-Geoffrion-Curry line and, led by Alex Delvecchio, skated to a 3-1 Cup-clinching victory. Maurice Richard could only watch as the Wings skated off with the Cup, and vowed that it would be his for the rest of his playing career.

TOP: *Gordie Howe scored the winning goal in Detroit's last Stanley Cup win, 14 April 1955.*

ABOVE: *Terry Sawchuk weeps tears of joy on the shoulder of Detroit general manager Jack Adams after the gruelling seven-game final in 1955.*

1956

Montreal vs Detroit

The Montreal Canadiens dominated the NHL in 1956, winning 45 games and finishing 24 points ahead of second place Detroit. Jacques Plante became the dominant goalie of the league and Jean Beliveau captured the scoring title. Montreal opened their semifinal series against the Rangers and, except for a brief letdown in game two, blasted the Blues back to their nest on the corner of 8th Avenue and 49th Street.

OPPOSITE: *George Armstrong puts the deke on Glenn Hall, with Bill Dineen in close pursuit. The Wings beat the Leafs in five games to reach the 1956 finals.*

ABOVE: *Ted Lindsay plays leap-frog with an obscured Jacques Plante as (l-r) Harvey, Pronovost and Howe pursue the puck.*

The other semifinal featured perennial rivals the Detroit Red Wings and the Toronto Maple Leafs. Detroit had no trouble with this youthful Leaf team, sending them back to Carlton and Church streets in five games.

This set up the third consecutive final series between the Wings and the Canadiens. Montreal had home ice advantage in this series, and put it to good use. Game one seemed to be comfortably in the hands of the Wings, but the Habs fired four unanswered third period goals to come from behind and win 6-4. This gave the Canadiens the confidence they required, and they rolled over the Wings 5-1 in game two. The action shifted to Detroit for the next two games, where Gordie Howe and Terrible Ted Lindsay each played outstanding games in a 3-1 Detroit conquest. Game four featured a remarkable performance by Jacques Plante, who shut out the Wings 3-0 to give the Canadiens a commanding lead in the best-of-seven. Game five started slowly but picked up momentum when the Canadiens scored a pair 52 seconds apart in the second period. The Habs added another quick one just seconds into the third period, and sent their ecstatic fans back onto Ste-Catherine Street with a Cup-clinching 3-1 performance.

RIGHT: *Gump Worsley gets help from Harry Howell (3) and Jack Evans as Henri Richard searches for a loose puck. The Habs beat the Rangers in five games to advance to the 1956 finals.*

1956

1957

Montreal vs Boston

The Detroit Red Wings returned to the top of the standings in this season, led by Gordie Howe's return to form and his league scoring title. They would go on to meet the Boston Bruins, who had had an outstanding season of their own. Montreal played the Rangers who had finished in fourth place, ahead of Toronto and Chicago.

The Bruins were the surprise of the regular season, and they continued their inspired play in the playoffs. Led by the goaltending of Don Simmons, they eliminated the Redbirds in five games and awaited the Montreal Canadiens, who fought off a determined effort by the Rangers.

The finals opened in Montreal, and Maurice Richard singlehandedly took game one. He fired four goals and was at his intimidating best as the Canadiens swamped the

Bears 5-1 in the opener. Game two belonged to Jacques Plante and Jean Beliveau. Plante whitewashed the Bruins and Beliveau scored the only goal in a 1-0 Montreal nailbiter. The teams moved to the den of the Bears for games three and four. Referee Eddie Powers had barely faced the opening draw when Boom Boom Geoffrion boomed one, giving the Canadiens a lead they would never relinquish. Montreal's 4-2 win put them in the driver's seat, but Boston flashed the red light to stop the Montreal joy ride. Fernie Flaman was the offensive star and Don Simmons the defensive hero in a 2-0 Bruin fan pleaser. Boston moved precariously into the fan-filled Forum for game five. The Canadiens' relentless attack left the Bruins scurrying for cover, and when the final whistle blew the hometown heroes held the Cup high and the scoreboard read Montreal 5, Boston 1.

1958

Montreal vs Boston

The 1958 version of Les Habitants de Montreal continued as the dominant force in the National Hockey League. Dickie Moore of the Canadiens was the scoring leader, followed closely by the Pocket Rocket, Henri Richard. Jacques Plante was the standout goaltender with nine shutouts and a goals-against average of 2.11. The Montreal Canadiens, first place finishers, met the third place Detroit Red Wings in the semifinals. The Canadiens were not in a pleasant mood when the series began, and proved it with a pasting of the Wings in four one-sided games. The Boston Bruins reached the finals for the second straight year, disposing of the New York Rangers in six games.

The Bruins did not have a spectacular season, but they were expected to give a better account of themselves than in the previous year. Game one was a wild affair. In the first period alone 14 penalties were called. They slashed, hooked, tripped and fought each other all the way into the third period. By this time, however, the Habs had potted two power play goals and held on to make them count in a 2-1 opener. The Bruins fought back hard in game two, out-scoring Montreal in the first period and cruising the rest of the way with a series-tying 5-2 conquest.

The teams journeyed to Beantown to continue the series, and the Richard brothers owned game three. The Pocket carried a pair of goals and the Rocket fired one as the Habs bested the Bears 3-0. The Bruins came out in game four firing on all cylinders. Scoring in each period, they tied up the series with a 3-1 victory. The fifth game was a nailbiter and a crowd pleaser. The teams traded goals in regulation play and needed extra time to settle the matter. When a game was on the line, there was always one man the Canadiens could look to. Maurice Richard took a pass from his kid brother and fired the goal that put the Canadiens one win shy of the Stanley Cup.

Montreal resembled the Flying Frenchmen of old in game six. The match was not two minutes old when the Canadiens had already registered a two-goal lead. They added two more in the second, allowed the Bruins to pull within one, then salted it away in the final minute for a dramatic 5-3 celebratory clincher. The Habs had now tied the Leafs with their third straight Stanley Cup conquest.

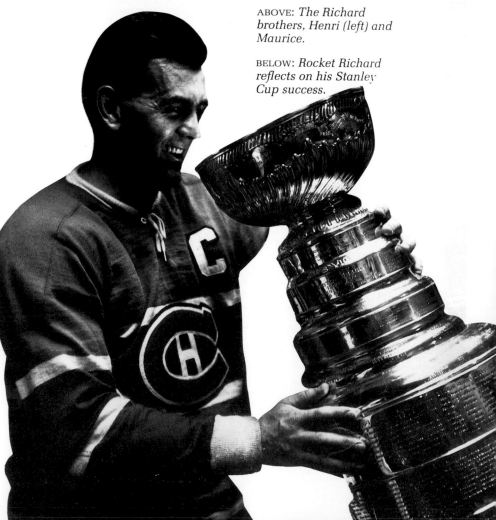

ABOVE: *The Richard brothers, Henri (left) and Maurice.*

BELOW: *Rocket Richard reflects on his Stanley Cup success.*

1959

Montreal vs Toronto

The Montreal Canadiens returned to the top of the standings in 1959 led by Dickie Moore, who set a new NHL mark with 96 points in the season. The Detroit Red Wings, who had dominated the standings during much of the decade, found themselves coming full circle, ending up in the NHL basement. The Habs were clear favourites to dispose of the Chicago Black Hawks in the semifinals, and they did not disappoint. Chicago gave a good account of themselves, but couldn't match the Montreal fire power and fell in six games.

The surprise of the season had to be the play of the Toronto Maple Leafs. Punch Imlach was the new coach, and he boldly predicted that not only would the Leafs defeat the Bruins in the semifinal, but whoever dared to meet them in the finals as well. Despite dropping the first two games, the Leafs stormed back to defeat the Bears in seven games and reach the finals for the first time since the infamous Barilko goal in 1951.

Game one in Montreal was an evenly matched contest. The teams were tied with eight minutes remaining when the Habs scored two quick goals to take the series lead with a 5-3 win. Montreal used third period fire power in game two as well, scoring two unanswered goals to send the series back to Toronto. The Leafs played up to Coach Imlach's expectations in the third

game, and won the match in overtime when Dickie Duff scored a pretty goal to cap off a 3-2 victory. Game four was scoreless until the third period. Billy Harris gave the Leafs a lead, but the Canadiens' attack began to pan out. In a six minute burst of power, Ab McDonald, Ralph Backstrom and Boom Boom Geoffrion all beat Johnny Bower and held on to win 3-2. The series returned to the Forum, where the Montreal Canadiens put their names into the record book. The Habs scored three first period goals and held the lead throughout, ending the Leaf's Cinderella season with a convincing 5-3 win and taking home their fourth straight Stanley Cup.

ABOVE: *Tom Johnson clears the puck from an on-rushing George Armstrong in a 3-2 Leaf victory during the 1959 finals.*

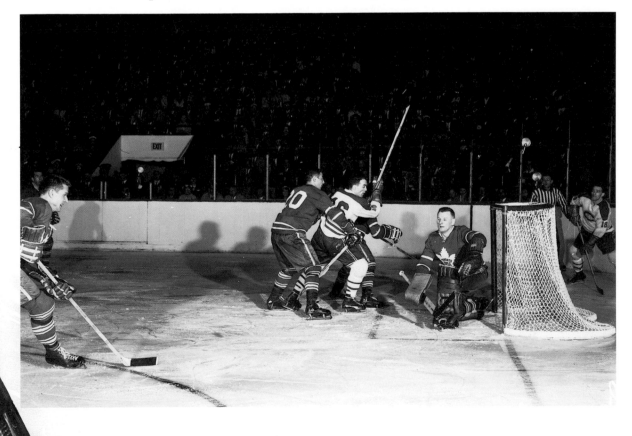

LEFT: *Bob Pulford (20) moves Henri Richard (16) from Johnny Bower's crease. Montreal beat the Leafs in five games to win their fourth straight Cup.*

1960

1960

Montreal vs Toronto

The 1960 season was dominated once again by the Montreal Canadiens. Jacques Plante won the Vezina Trophy, becoming the first masked goaltender to turn that trick. There was plenty of excitement in the final days of the season as the Hawks, Wings and Bruins all battled for a playoff spot and seven players fought it out for the league's scoring title. The Canadiens met the Chicago Black Hawks in the semifinals and dispensed with the Hawks quickly and painlessly. The Toronto Maple Leafs fought a determined Detroit Red Wings team and made their second straight appearance in the finals after eliminating the Motor City Wings in a six-game semi.

The Habs and the Leafs met once again in the finals. The Leafs' youth building project had reaped great benefits. Frank Mahovlich, the 1958 Rookie of the Year, and Bob Pulford were the offensive stars, while a veteran blueline crew of Bobby Baun, Allan Stanley and Tim Horton made 38-year-old Johnny Bower's net minding look easy. The Leafs would be no match for the Habs, however. Montreal stormed out of the gate with three goals all masterminded by Henri Richard. Richard added one of his own in the third period, and the Canadiens took the series lead with a 4-2 triumph. The Canadiens were first out of the gate in the second game as well, scoring two goals before the game was six minutes old. The defence took over for the rest of the game, allowing just one Toronto tally and, with this 2-1 win behind them, the Habs headed to Toronto.

Game three was more of the same with the Canadiens scoring first, opening up a large lead and holding on for a 5-2 victory. The fifth Montreal goal was scored when Maurice Richard picked up a loose puck in front of the Toronto target and fired it over the shoulder of Johnny Bower. This was the last goal Maurice Richard would score in his illustrious career. Montreal's momentum was unstoppable in game four, as they scored two goals in a 30-second span during the first period. Single goals by Henri Richard and Jean Beliveau in the second and third periods wrapped up the Cup for the greatest dynasty in NHL history.

The glory days of the Montreal Canadiens were behind them. Maurice Richard retired at the end of the season, and although he was only the greatest of what was a great team, his loss would shake the Habs to the core. Today, his name is hard to find in the record book, but he dominated his game and his sport with an intensity that record books cannot convey.

OPPOSITE TOP: *George Armstrong can't corral this loose puck in front of Plante, as the Habs beat the Leafs 5-2, 12 April 1960.*

OPPOSITE BOTTOM: *Doug Harvey wheels away from Leaf pursuers Duff and Armstrong.*

LEFT: *A weary Jacques Plante and Maurice Richard grasp their fifth consecutive Stanley Cup after blanking Toronto in the game and series 4-0, 14 April 1960.*

1961

ABOVE: *The 'Golden Jet,' Bobby Hull, was the third man in NHL history to score 50 goals in one season.*

TOP RIGHT: *Billy Reay, the last man to coach the Hawks to a Stanley Cup victory, 16 April 1961.*

Chicago vs Detroit

The year 1961 was one of the more exciting years in the history of the National Hockey League. The introduction of network hockey broadcasting was bringing the game to more people across Canada and the United States than ever before. The influx of new talent, including Bobby Hull, Frank Mahovlich, Stan Mikita and Davey Keon, was giving the game a new crop of heroes for the television generation.

The highlight of the regular season was the intense battle between Frank Mahovlich of the Leafs and Montreal's Boom Boom Geoffrion to reach the 50-goal plateau. The Big M led this competition throughout most of the season, but tailed off during the final games of the campaign. Geoffrion picked up the spark and, on 16 March in a game against Toronto, he became the second man in

history to score 50 goals in a single season. Boom Boom's offensive output helped the Canadiens to the regular season title, and they prepared to meet the Chicago Black Hawks in the first round of their bid for six consecutive Stanley Cups.

Chicago pulled off the upset of their history in this series. Led by the Golden Jet, Bobby Hull, and the goaltending of Glenn Hall, they eliminated the Habs in six games. The other semifinal also saw a major upset. The Detroit Red Wings finished 24 points behind Toronto, and mustered all their resources to overthrow them in the semifinal round.

Fans had gotten used to seeing the Montreal Canadiens in April, since they had been on the ice for the final round for the last ten years. Now, for the first time since 1950, two American teams would compete in the Stanley Cup finals.

The first game was played in Chicago, where Bobby Hull scored a pair of goals to lead the Hawks to a 3-2 victory. In game two, played in Detroit, Alex Delvecchio matched that number in a 3-1 Detroit win. The teams alternated cities for each game, using up a lot of player steam power just getting from place to place. The next two decisions were split as well, 3-1 Chicago and 2-1 Detroit. Game five was played in Chicago and the teams were tied after two periods. Stan Mikita took control of the game in the third, scoring two goals and setting up another. With this 6-3 victory Chicago was one game away from their first Stanley Cup since 1938. Detroit scored the first goal in game six, but it was the last one they would record until next year's training camp. The Hawks put on a sharp-shooting display for the Motown fans and scored five goals in succession. In what was a true team effort, the Chicago Black Hawks had arrived at the Stanley Cup winner's circle.

1962

Toronto vs Chicago

Montreal retained their league pennant in 1962, but much of the attention was focussed on Chicago's Bobby Hull. It was his turn to take home the Art Ross Trophy, which he secured in the final game of the season when he scored his fiftieth goal. The Habs' first place finish guaranteed them a place in the semifinals, where they faced the defending Cup champion Chicago Black Hawks. Montreal's fine season came to a close when they fell to the Hawks in six games. As America circled the globe in space, the Golden Jet hoped that he could fuel the Hawks' bid for a space age hockey dynasty.

The Toronto Maple Leafs reached the finals for the third time in four years, overcoming a determined New York Ranger team in six games. The Chicago defence of the Cup began on 10 April in Maple Leaf Gardens. The first game was a rough, penalty-filled encounter. Bobby Hull opened the scoring for Chicago, but from there on it was all Toronto. The Leafs, led by Mahovlich and Keon, counted four consec-

utive goals and took the contest 4-1. Game two was a much tamer affair. Billy Harris scored a power play goal for the Leafs in the first period and George Armstrong tallied the winner in the third as the Leafs headed to Chicago up two games in the series. The Hawks turned the tables on the Leafs in their hometown games, shutting them out 3-0 in the third game and outscoring and outfighting them 4-1 in the fourth.

The series shifted back to Toronto and the flood gates opened in game five. The Leafs pounded eight goals past Glenn Hall, tripping the Hawks 8-4. The teams returned to Chicago Stadium and played much tighter, more defensive hockey. There was no scoring until the third period when Bobby Hull blasted one past Don Simmons in the Leaf net. The Leafs' Bob Nevin quickly got that one back, and Tim Horton set up the winner by Dick Duff after an impressive end-to-end rush. Months earlier the remains of Bill Barilko had been found in a heavily wooded area of northern Ontario, putting to an end the ten years of Leafs' mourning for the fallen hero. Toronto defeated Chicago to win their first Stanley Cup in a decade.

BELOW: *Carl Brewer (2) deflects this shot from the Hawks' Murray Balfour in the opening game of the 1962 finals. The Hawks won this battle 3-0, but the Leafs won the war four games to two.*

BELOW: *A joyous group of Leafs: (L-r) Simmons, Baun, Imlach, Stanley, Duff and Kelly celebrate their first Cup victory in 11 years, 22 April 1962.*

1963

ABOVE: *(L-r) Ullman, Gadsby, Keon, Pulford and Sawchuk look for the puck, but no one seems to know where it is. During the 1963 finals it ended up in the Detroit cage more than in the Leafs' as Toronto won the Cup in five game.*

Toronto vs Detroit

The pursuit of the NHL pennant in this season featured a gruelling four-team race, and when the curtain fell on the regular campaign only five points separated the playoff contenders. The Toronto Maple Leafs finished in the top spot and readied themselves to greet the Montreal Canadiens in the semifinals. The ensuing five-game set was characterised by tight-checking, 'old-time' hockey. The goaltending of Johnny Bower was the deciding factor in the Leafs' five-game success, and assured the Buds of the chance to defend the Cup.

Gordie Howe returned to the top of the leader board in the scoring race, and he rallied his Detroit Red Wings against the Chicago Black Hawks in the other semifinal. The Wings rebounded after losing the first two matches and reached the finals with a full head of steam, eager to unseat the defending champs.

The first encounter showed the Leafs in fine form. Dick Duff fired two goals in the first minute, and Bob Nevin added a brace as the home side skated over the Wings 4-2 in the opener. The Leafs came out flying in the return match as well, opening with a three-goal flurry, then barring the door in another

4-2 conquest. Detroit cut a game off of the Leaf lead in the third contest, played on their home turf. Led by the unheralded (and unheard of) Alex Faulkner, the Wings managed to sneak past the Leafs in a 3-2 crowd pleaser.

Game four was highlighted by the acrobatics of Johnny Bower, who gave ample proof that his moniker, the China Wall, was well-deserved. He made several outstanding stops, mostly off the blade of Gordie Howe, to keep the Leafs in the game. His spot on the hero's podium was shared by Dave Keon, whose two unassisted goals in the final frame put the Leafs back in the driver's seat with a 4-2 triumph. Back home in the House that Smythe Built, the Leafs and Wings treated the Toronto faithful to a tremendous display of playoff entertainment. The issue was in doubt until the waning moments, when the Entertainer, Eddie Shack, stepped into the spotlight. With six minutes to go, a bouncing puck struck a Detroit Red Wings player, then hit a well-positioned Shack, and somehow found a home in the back of the Detroit cage. Dave Keon added an empty-net goal, and the Leafs were guaranteed a parade up Bay Street as Stanley Cup Champions for the second consecutive year.

1964

Toronto vs Detroit

The same four clubs involved in the 1963 playoffs also qualified for postseason play in 1964. In fact, the match-ups would be the same, although Montreal and Toronto would reverse spots in the standings, the Habs ending up as season titlists. Chicago were bridesmaids again, finishing one point behind the Canadiens but featuring the fire power to make a great deal of noise in the playoffs.

Bolstered by the one-two punch of Bobby Hull and Stan Mikita, Chicago met the Detroit Red Wings in the semifinals, and although the Hawks looked stronger on paper, the game is played on ice. Detroit, led by such playoff veterans as Howe, Delvecchio, Gadsby, Ullman and Pronovost, ignored the betting line and fought the Hawks to a seventh game, then sent the Golden Jet and company home for an early vacation.

The other semifinal also featured a seven-game marathon, with the defending champion Leafs earning their third straight shot at the Silver Mug after putting Montreal on the sidelines. Toronto used third period heroics from George Armstrong and Bob Pulford (who scored with two seconds remaining) to pull off the first match of the finals by a count of 3-2. The Leafs needed a last-minute marker from Gerry Ehman to force overtime in game two, but Larry Jeffrey notched a sudden-death goal for Detroit to send the teams to Motown on even terms. Detroit came out smoking in game three, and when Floyd Smith's wrist shot found net, the Wings had built an early 3-0 advantage. The Leafs fought back, securing a tie when Don McKenney beat Sawchuk with 70 seconds left in the third period. The Wings avoided overtime, however, thanks to a timely shot by Alex Delvecchio with only a handful of ticks left on the timeclock.

Toronto pulled even in game four, potting three unanswered goals in a 4-2 victory, but found themselves on the brink of elimination after a 2-1 loss in game five. The sixth game belonged to the courageous Bob Baun. With the affair tied at 3-3, the clubs went into sudden-death. Baun picked up a pass from Bob Pulford, skirted the blueline, and flipped a shot that went through a maze of players and into the Detroit net. Only after the fact was it disclosed that Baun had played the last portion of the game on a broken leg. The Leafs, fuelled by Baun's determination, shut out the Wings 4-0 in game seven and hoisted the Cup onto Coach Imlach's shoulders for the third consecutive season.

BELOW: *Johnny Bower slaps this shot from Parker McDonald (20) out of harm's way as Bobby Baun (21) clears the crease, 23 April 1964. Baun later scored in overtime of this sixth game, and the Leafs would go on to win the seven-game final for their third straight Cup.*

1965

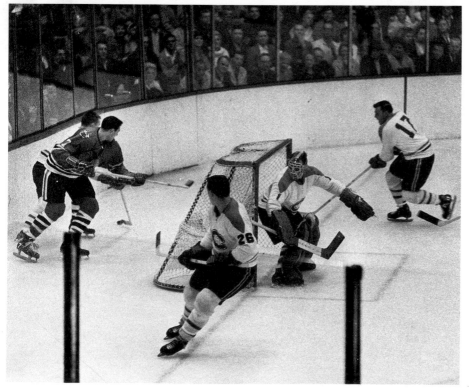

Montreal vs Chicago

After seven years in the Hall of Mediocrity, the Detroit Red Wings rose to the top of the NHL standings in 1965, their main source of fire power being Norm Ullman, whose 42 goals led the NHL. Stan Mikita of the Chicago Black Hawks won his second Art Ross Trophy, and the Boston Bruins missed the playoffs for the sixth straight year.

Despite the shift in the standings, the semifinal match-ups yielded the same contenders as in the past three years. The Chicago Black Hawks faced off against Detroit, and after seven determined matches, and eight goals by Bobby Hull, they were ready for the final round. In the other semifinal, the Toronto Maple Leafs were matched against their Canadian rivals in Montreal. The Canadiens got the better of Toronto in this series and raked the Leafs away for the summer in six games.

When the finals opened in Montreal, it marked a special moment for Hab goalie Gump Worsley. After 12 years of wearing the 'tools of ignorance,' 36-year-old Worsley made his first appearance in a Stanley Cup final. The Habs established a trend that would be followed throughout the course of the series by winning the home games 3-2 and 2-0. The scene shifted to the confines of Chicago Stadium, where the Hawks used third period magic to tie the series by 3-1 and 5-1 scores.

Worsley recorded his second shutout of the set in game five. Jean Beliveau scored a pair and set up a pair in the Canadiens' 6-0 romp. Game six was a brutal encounter, but the Hawks prevailed 2-1 and forced a deciding seventh game, back in the Forum. The Habs left the dressing room flying, Jean Beliveau scoring at the 14-second mark and Bobby Rousseau assisting on three of the four Montreal first period markers. The Habs shut the door the rest of the way, giving the Gumper his third zero of the finals and the fans of Montreal their first Cup since 1960.

Jean Beliveau was awarded the first Conn Smythe Trophy, a new award donated by the architect of the Toronto Maple Leafs, and presented to the MVP of the playoffs.

ABOVE LEFT: *The Conn Smythe Trophey.*

LEFT: *Hawks 5, Habs 1, 25 April 1965.*

OPPOSITE: *Jean Beliveau (4) battles Stan Mikita (21), Cup finals, 1965.*

1966

Montreal vs Detroit

Fans in 1966 were electrified by the scoring wizardry of Bobby Hull. This sure bet for the Hall of Fame won worldwide media attention when, on 12 March, he drove a shot past New York's Cesare Maniago to break Maurice Richard's record of 50 goals in a season. Hull's performance won him both the Art Ross and Hart trophies. His Chicago Black Hawks finished in second place, and met the Detroit Red Wings in the semifinals.

The Hawks had defeated the Wings 11 times in the regular season, but the playoffs are another thing entirely. Detroit outscored the Hawks 22-10 in six games, sending a shocked group of Hawks to the dressing room for the last time that year. It was war on ice in the other semifinal. The Montreal Canadiens and the Maple Leafs set a number of penalty records during a four-game sweep by the defending champs.

ABOVE: *Jubilation: Hawks vs. Habs, Cup finals, 1966.*

RIGHT: *Leon Rochefort (25) scores for Montreal in game six of the Cup finals, 5 May 1966.*

1966

OPPOSITE TOP: *Bobby Rousseau (15) drives the net, watched by Bruce McGregor and goalie Roger Crozier.*

OPPOSITE BOTTOM: *(L-r) Henderson, Ullman, Gadsby and McGregor clear the puck, Cup finals, 1966.*

BELOW: *Le Butte!! Habs vs. Wings, Cup finals, 1966.*

The first two games in Montreal were won by Detroit, thanks to spectacular goaltending by Roger Crozier. When the games shifted to Detroit, the scoring shifted to the Habs. Gilles Tremblay netted two goals in less than two minutes to shift the tide and give the Habs a 4-2 victory in game three. The Detroit fans watched in horror as Roger Crozier was rammed into the goalpost in the first period of game four. He was helped from the ice and was not to return in this game. Montreal took control shortly thereafter, and after Ralph Backsrom fired a Dickie Duff pass beyond the reach of Hank Bassen, the series was tied.

Crozier returned to the nets for game five, but it was obvious that he was not one hundred percent. The Canadiens opened up a quick 4-0 lead and made it stand up in a 5-1 tie breaker. Game six was back in the Motor City. Montreal led 2-0 but Detroit stormed back, tying it midway through the third. The game was in sudden death overtime when Henri Richard stole a page from his famous brother's playbook and slipped, slid and slapped the puck past Roger Crozier and into the history books. Richard's bizarre blueline-to-goal-line slide brought the Montreal Canadiens their seventh Stanley Cup in the last ten years.

The dramatic goaltending of Roger Crozier earned him the nod as Conn Smythe Trophy winner, but it was a poor substitute for Lord Stanley's own Mug.

1967

Toronto vs Montreal

In one of the more dramatic turns of form, Stan Mikita captured not only the Art Ross Trophy and the Hart Trophy, but the Lady Byng Trophy as well. The now gentlemanly Mikita dropped from 154 penalty minutes in 1965, to only 12 minutes in the sin bin in 1967. He became the first triple crown winner in NHL history.

The Chicago Black Hawks not only outscored their opponents by a large margin, but allowed the fewest goals as well, winning the league flag by 17 points. They met the Toronto Maple Leafs in the first playoff round, and were expected to have no trouble with Punch Imlach's troupe of old-timers. No one, especially Chicago fans, was prepared for the outcome. The Leafs, who experts felt were better suited to summer hockey schools than NHL arenas, gave the pundits a healthy slice of humble pie. This squad of solid veterans saw the writing on the wall: This was to be their last hurrah, and they feasted on Black Birds in a six-game win.

The New York Rangers reached the playoffs for the first time in five years, but gave the defending champion Canadiens little trouble and were swept from the playoffs in straight games.

It was only fitting that in Canada's centen-

nial year, the two Canadian franchises should celebrate the birthday with a party of their own. Game one was held in Montreal, at the height of the World's Fair, and tickets were at an absolute premium. The world came to the birthday bash, and the Leafs and Canadiens did not disappoint. Henri Richard stepped into the spotlight and fired a hat trick as the Canadiens opened the series with a 6-2 win. The second game belonged to the 'old man' of the Leafs, Johnny Bower. He slammed the door and refused to open it, as the Leafs tied the series with a 3-0 exhibition. Game three was a real goaltender's duel. Rogie Vachon, the rookie goaltender who Punch Imlach referred to as 'that Junior B kid,' faced 62 shots, while his worthy opponent Johnny Bower saw 54. The teams were tied at twos when the final tick of the clock signalled the end of regulation time. They were still tied 28 minutes later when Bob Pulford scored a dramatic overtime marker to give the Leafs the lead in the series.

Game four started on a bad note for the Leafs. Johnny Bower was injured in the pre-game warmup and would be lost for the rest of the series. Terry Sawchuk, who had joined the Leafs as a backup in 1965, was forced into the fray. The Canadiens took advantage of the rusty veteran and evened the series with a 6-2 thrashing of the Leafs. Toronto fans groaned when Sawchuk allowed an early goal in game five, but he reversed the Habs' onslaught and shut them out the rest of the way as the Leafs took command of the series with a 4-1 victory. The Leafs knew, as they paraded onto the Gardens ice for game six, that this must be their night. They couldn't chance another journey back to Montreal.

Sawchuk was magnificent as he held the Habs off the scoresheet in the first 40 minutes. Ron Ellis and Jim Pappin, with second period tallies, gave the Leafs a 2-0 advantage, but the affair was tightened significantly when Dick Duff countered for the Habs in the third. With less than a minute remaining, the Habs forced a face-off in the Leaf zone, and pulled their goalie for an extra attacker. Imlach sent his five most experienced defenders onto the ice: Horton, Armstrong, Pulford, Stanley and Kelly. Captain Armstrong secured the puck, fired it the length of the pond into the empty cage and the Leafs had won the Stanley Cup. Dave Keon was selected as the MVP and took the Conn Smythe Trophy.

1967

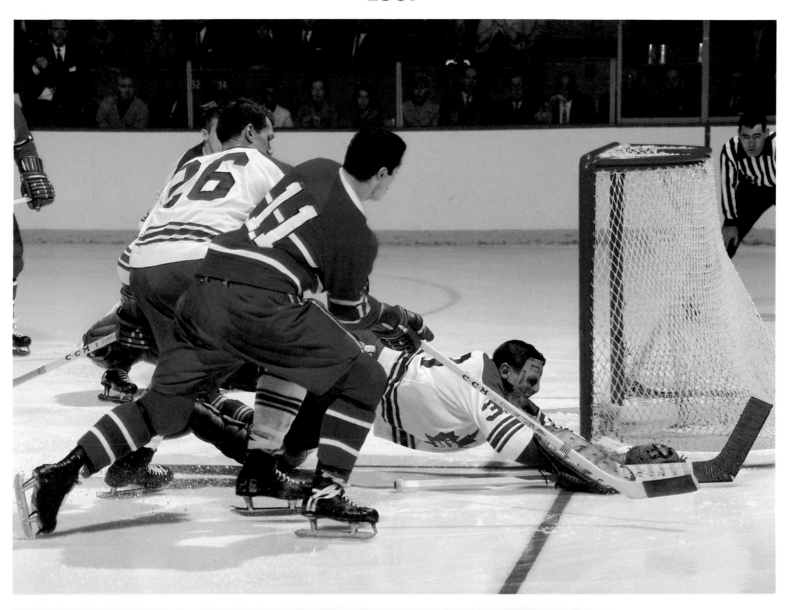

ABOVE: *Terry Sawchuk dives to smother the puck with Claude Larose on the doorstep, Stanley Cup finals, 1967. Sawchuk's famed 'pinch-hitting' role in the 1967 series was the last great highlight of his career.*

OPPOSITE: *Leaf captain Dave Keon battles Guy Lafleur for possession of the puck. The Leafs-Canadiens rivalry is the most renowned in Stanley Cup history.*

LEFT: *Rogie Vachon manages to get a pad on this drive off the stick of Jim Pappin (18) in the 1967 Cup finals. Pappin would get his revenge, leading the pack in scoring, and tallying the Cup winner for Toronto.*

1968

Montreal vs St. Louis

The National Hockey League entered a new era in 1968, when teams from St. Louis, Los Angeles, Oakland, Minnesota, Pittsburgh and Philadelphia joined the circuit. These six new clubs formed a division of their own, and the winner of this West Division was guaranteed a challenge for the Stanley Cup. Amid the optimism which greeted this expansion came one tragic note. Bill Masterton, who had come out of retirement to join the Minnesota North Stars, became the first player in NHL history to lose his life as a

1968

direct result of an on-ice injury.

The Montreal Canadiens defeated the Boston Bruins and Chicago Black Hawks to earn a berth in the finals, while in the West Division the St. Louis Blues played down the Philadelphia Flyers and Minnesota North Stars to find their way to the Forum.

The St. Louis team, like many of the expansion clubs, were a rag-tag group of veterans and inexperienced rookies. They had acquired Dickie Moore, Jean-Guy Talbot and Noel Picard from the Montreal Canadiens, and this trio had extensive playoff experience. Their greatest asset was between

BELOW: *Canadiens Gump Worsley and Yvon Cournoyer (12) combine to halt the Bruins' Derek Sanderson during the 1968 semifinals.*

1968

LEFT: *Canadien Ralph Backstrom (6) is tackled by the Blues' Bob Plager (5) and Red Berenson (7), while Doug Harvey (2) and Glenn Hall (1) look on. The St. Louis team, though swept in four games, was in every contest until the final whistle. Each game was decided by one goal, with the Habs needing overtime in games one and three to make the St. Louis fans sing the blues.*

BELOW LEFT: *Jacques Lemaire (25) parks himself in front of the Blues cage and awaits a behind-the-net pass from teammate Bobby Rousseau. Lemaire fired seven goals in the 1968 playoffs, including the overtime winner in game one of the finals.*

the pipes, where Glenn Hall presided.

The Blues were given no chance to defeat the powerful Canadiens, and Montreal appeared to be overconfident as the series

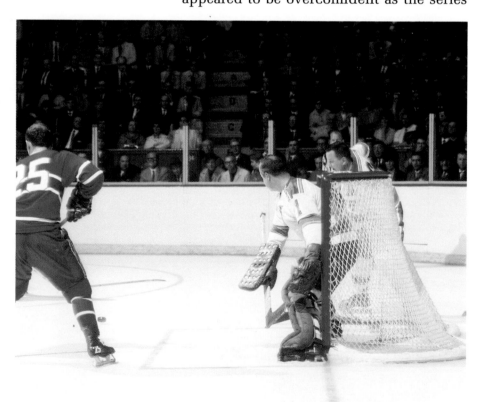

began. St. Louis matched the Habs goal for goal in game one, forcing the match into overtime. The St. Louis prayers for a miracle came up short as Jacques Lemaire blasted a shot past Hall to give the Habs the series lead. Game two was scoreless until the third period. Gump Worsley was outstanding for the home side and his play enabled Serge Savard's short-handed marker to stand as the winning goal in a 1-0 crowd pleaser. The St. Louis fans savoured their first taste of live Stanley Cup final action in game three. The Blues again delivered a brave performance, but once again the Canadiens prevailed in overtime. Bobby Rousseau fired the winner to give the Habs a 4-3 win, and an insurmountable lead in the series.

St. Louis battled the Habs again in game four, but lacked the seasoning and stamina to overcome the Montreal attack. J. C. Tremblay scored late in the third period, and the Montreal Canadiens returned to the winner's podium with a 3-2 victory.

St. Louis had not won a game, but had shown the detractors that expansion hockey could keep pace. The Conn Smythe Trophy was awarded to Glenn Hall of St. Louis, whose stellar performance kept the Blues within one goal in each game.

1969

Montreal vs St. Louis

For the first time since 1955, the Montreal Canadiens entered the season with a new coach. Hector 'Toe' Blake had retired from the bench, but had left with no less than 11 Stanley Cup rings. His successor, Claude Ruel, rallied the troops and the Canadiens repeated as East Division champions. The Habs swept past the Rangers and defeated an aggressive Boston Bruin team to earn their fifth straight shot at Stanley Cup silver. The status quo in the West Division remained in the hands of the St. Louis Blues. They had convinced Jacques Plante to return to active play, and he combined with Glenn Hall to win the Vezina Trophy. St. Louis' stubborn defence allowed them to sweep past both Philadelphia and L.A., earning a return to the Stanley Cup finals.

The series opened at 'Hockey Central' in Montreal. Dick Duff and Bob Rousseau tallied 48 seconds apart in the first period and Bad John Ferguson added an empty-netter as the Canadiens continued their dominance over the Blues with a 3-1 victory. St. Louis had more trouble in game two and the Canadiens opened up a 3-0 lead by the midway point of the second period. The St. Louis offence could not get on track and they dropped the game by an identical 3-1 count. This lack of offensive punch continued into the third game. The Habs, behind Rogie Vachon, blanked the Blues 4-0. St. Louis tried a new, more aggressive game plan in game five, and it was going

well when St. Louis entered the third period with a 1-0 lead. The Canadiens were spending playoff cash in their minds, and Ted Harris and John Ferguson deposited the cash in Habitant accounts with two speedy third period goals.

The Canadiens had captured yet another 'Coupe de Stanley,' and for Claude Ruel it marked the eleventh time a rookie coach had won the big hockey silverware. Serge Savard, the big, aggressive blueliner, became the first defenceman to win the Conn Smythe Trophy.

ABOVE: *St. Louis defenders Al Arbour (3), Bob Plager (5) and Bill McCreary (15) surround the 'Roadrunner,' Yvon Cournoyer.*

LEFT: *Henri Richard finds the going tough along the boards as Doug Harvey (2) and Ron Schock (10) combine to press him.*

1970

Boston vs St. Louis

The year 1970 was the year of Bobby Orr. This well-heeled kid out of the northern Ontario backwater of Parry Sound was to revolutionise the playbook for defencemen. Orr joined the Bruins' big team in 1966-67, and as Rookie of the Year gave a preview of the show that would really begin in 1969-70. For the first time, and to the utter amazement of scribes and scholars, this rushing defenceman won not only the Norris Trophy, but the Art Ross as well. He tallied 33 goals and a record-breaking 87 assists for a point count of 120. This remarkable young man nearly singlehandedly put the Boston Bruins into the final round of Stanley Cup action.

In the West Division, for the third straight year St. Louis reached the Stanley Cup

finals, overcoming Minnesota and Pittsburgh to obtain the ticket. Boston took out New York and Chicago to earn their place in the Cup finals.

For the first time since 1958, the Boston fans were treated to the excitement of a Stanley Cup final match. St. Louis held the Bruins to two goals through the first 40 minutes, but the powerful Boston attack led by Derek Sanderson and Johnny Bucyk exploded for four goals in the final 20 minutes for a 6-1 win. Eddie Westfall led the Bruins in game two, scoring a brace of first period goals as the Bruins continued their march toward the Cup. Bobby Orr was a defensive standout as the Bruins dominated the Blues 6-2.

Wayne Cashman led the Bears in game three. This career Boston Bruin attacker who scored only nine goals in the regular campaign blasted two in the third period, securing a 4-1 decision. St. Louis managed to slow down the Boston offensive blitz in game four while mounting an attack of their own in building a 3-2 advantage. Johnny Bucyk broke through the St. Louis defence to tie the game at threes and send it into sudden death. Bobby Orr, who had been held goalless in the preceding three games, redirected a pass from Derek Sanderson past a sprawling Glenn Hall to give Boston their first Stanley Cup in 29 years. The image of Orr flying through the air after scoring the winning goal is one of the most memorable photos in Stanley Cup lore.

Orr's prowess above and beyond his blueline earned him the final recognition available to a skater on a Stanley Cup team, and he added the Conn Smythe Trophy to his 1970 collection.

OPPOSITE TOP: *(L-r) Phil Esposito (with the Hart Trophy), Clarence Campbell (presenting the Art Ross Trophy) and Bobby Orr (with the Norris Trophy), 25 January 1970.*

OPPOSITE BOTTOM: *Bobby Orr begins his in-flight celebration after scoring the Cup-winning goal in overtime, 10 May 1970.*

BELOW: *Bobby Orr scores against Tony Esposito on his way to helping the Bruins sweep the Hawks in the Cup semifinals, 21 April 1970.*

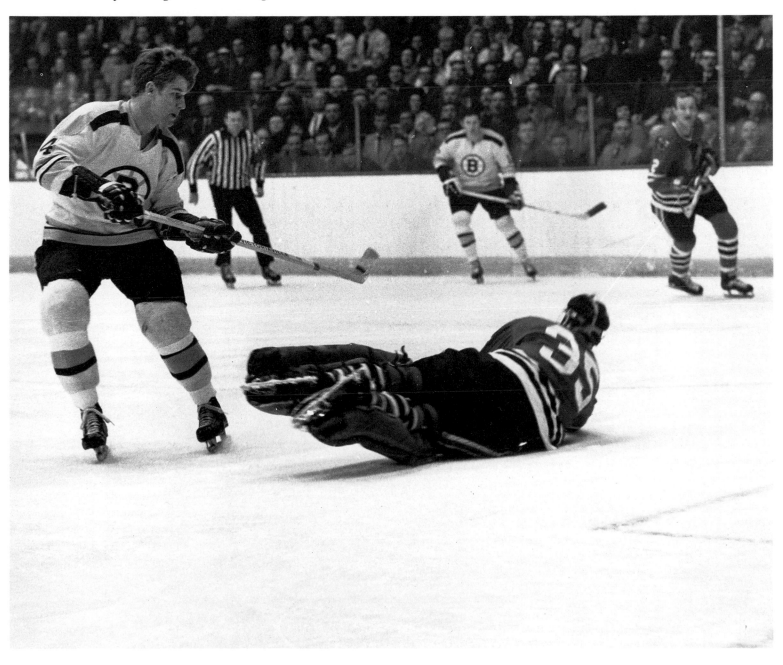

— **1971** —

Montreal vs Chicago

The NHL expanded again in 1971, adding the Buffalo Sabres and Vancouver Canucks to the fold. This forced a divisional realignment and a restructuring of the playoff format. The Chicago Black Hawks were added to the West Division in an attempt to create parity between the East and the West. The playoff format was altered, now featuring a crossover between divisions in the semifinals.

Chicago easily dominated their division, finishing 21 points ahead of St. Louis. Their march towards the finals was slightly more difficult. After dumping the Philadelphia Flyers in four straight, the Hawks had their hands full with the New York Rangers, the set going the full seven matches until the Hawks pushed past the Broadway Blues and into the finals.

The East Division featured an outstanding year by the Boston Bruins. The Beantowners set 34 team and NHL records, and had the top four scorers in the league. Phil Esposito crushed all scoring records with 76 goals and 152 points, and Bobby Orr set a new record with 102 assists. The Bruins felt that their defence of the Cup was a mere formality, and entered their series with the Montreal Canadiens brimming with overconfidence. The Habs, who had missed the playoffs the previous season, were anxious to erase that bitter memory, and they did so in spades. The Canadiens dealt the Bruins a crushing blow, taking out the critics' favourites in seven games, then marched past Minnesota into the Stanley Cup finals.

Montreal had two new faces in their lineup for the playoffs. Detroit dealt them Frank Mahovlich at midseason, and the Big M was a key factor in the Habs' defeat of the Bruins. The spotlight, however, belonged to a rookie goalie from the AHL. The Canadiens had called up Ken Dryden from the minors late in the season, and his performance against the Bruins remains the most remarkable debut in NHL history.

The finals began in Chicago, and the Hawks slowed the Hab express with an exciting double-overtime win in game one, thanks to the accuracy of Jim Pappin's dramatic game winner. The Hawks, with Lou Angotti and Bobby Hull leading the way, took a two-game lead with a 5-3 victory in the second match. Ken Dryden returned to form and continued his heroics in games

three and four. The Canadiens fought back to tie the series with 4-2 and 5-2 wins. Tony Esposito shut out the Habs in game five, but the Mahovlich brothers (Pete and Frank) kept Montreal's hopes alive, scoring key third period markers in a 4-3 Canadien win in game six. The classic game seven confrontation was decided by Henri Richard, who scored both the tying and winning goals in helping Montreal to upset Chicago and win the Cup.

Frank Mahovlich set playoff records for goals and points, but no one could argue that Ken Dryden's performance deserved the highest playoff accolade, the Conn Smythe Trophy.

ABOVE: *Frank Mahovlich, leading scorer in the 1971 playoffs.*

OPPOSITE: *Ken Dryden in a familiar pose.*

BELOW: *Montreal vs. Chicago, 1971 Cup finals.*

1972

RIGHT: *The 'Chief,' Bruin captain John Bucyk. Bucyk played 23 seasons in the NHL, all but 11 games of which were with the Boston Bruins.*

BELOW: *Bobby Orr clears the puck from Pete Stemkowski (21) with Esposito (7), McKenzie (19) and Johnston (1) offering verbal encouragement in game five of the 1972 Stanley Cup finals.*

Boston vs New York

The Boston Bruins and Chicago Black Hawks continued their dominance of their respective divisions. Phil Esposito won the scoring title once again, followed closely by teammate Bobby Orr. Bobby Hull scored 50 goals in the season, and Tony Esposito, with a goals-against average of 1.72, led all NHL netminders.

Boston crushed Toronto four games to one, then swept past St. Louis in four straight to arrive at the finals for the second time in three years. The New York Rangers, who had the third, fourth and fifth leading scorers in the NHL, defeated the defending champion Montreal Canadiens in six

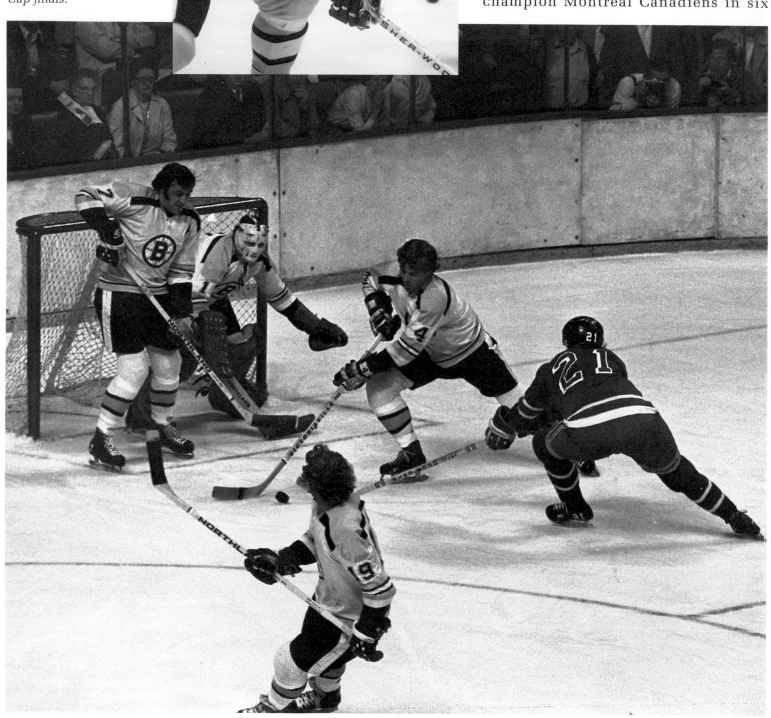

games, then swept the Hawks in four. This set up a confrontation between two teams which had not met in a final round since 1929, when Boston took home the prized silverware.

Game one was played, in wide open fashion, on Boston Gardens ice. When the ice was cleared and the score sheet totalled, Boston, thanks to a goal by Garnet (Ace) Bailey, had taken the lead in the series with a 6-5 win. Game two was a defensive three periods, but again Boston came out the winner 2-1. The Rangers used three first period power play goals to overcome the Bruins with a 5-2 victory in game three. The Bruins

rallied in game four, with Bobby Orr scoring two and setting up another in a 3-2 Boston squeaker. The Rangers kept the Mug off the Boston shelf in game five. Ranger Bobby Rousseau scored two third period goals, sending the series back to New York for game six. Gerry Cheevers assured the Bruins of another trip to the winner's circle, slamming the door on the Rangers in a 3-0 Cup-clinching whitewash.

Bobby Orr once again was acknowledged as the series' outstanding player, and was awarded the Conn Smythe Trophy. Orr was the first player to have won this honour on more than one occasion.

ABOVE: *Gerry Cheevers, wearing his infamous 'stitched' mask, watches as Bobby Orr (4) clears a rebound from an onrushing Brad Park (2) of the N.Y. Rangers, Cup finals, 1972. Brad Park appeared in the playoffs in 17 consecutive seasons, an NHL record. Ironically, despite never missing the postseason in his career, he never played on a Cup winner.*

OPPOSITE: *The Rangers offer congratulations to the Bruins following Boston's Cup victory in game six, 11 May 1972.*

ABOVE LEFT: *Phil Esposito (here battling with the Rangers' Walt Tkaczuk) led all playoff scorers in goals (9) and points (24) in 1972.*

ABOVE: *Derek Sanderson (16) races Vic Hadfield (11) for Stanley Cup glory, Cup finals, 1972.*

LEFT: *Dallas Smith (20) robs Bruce McGregor (14) of the puck, Cup finals, 1972.*

1973

Montreal vs Chicago

For the first time since the demise of the Pacific Coast Hockey Association, a first division professional hockey league was in competition with the NHL. The World Hockey Association would never compete for the Stanley Cup, but was in many ways important to the future progress of the game. They raided the NHL and paid their help salaries never dreamed of by NHL skaters. The new league was not taken seriously until some of the NHL's biggest stars defected to claim their share of the big money. Bobby Hull, Derek Sanderson, Bernie Parent and Gerry Cheevers are just a few of the big names that emblazoned the backs of WHA jerseys.

Montreal unseated Boston from the top of the East Division standings, but Chicago retained their number one seat in the West. Montreal defeated Buffalo in six games and Philadelphia in five, while the New York Rangers had their revenge against Boston vindicated in five games, but were stopped by Chicago in the semifinal round.

The finals between Montreal and Chicago featured the two outstanding goaltenders in the NHL facing each other. Tony Esposito of the Black Birds and Ken Dryden of the Habs

had been teammates on Team Canada in 1972, but now opposed each other for the biggest prize of all. Game one, played in Montreal, belonged to the Montreal Canadiens who fired eight pucks past Esposito in an 8-3 thrashing. Montreal had their way with the Hawks in game two as well, using Yvon Cournoyer's two goals to assure a 4-1 victory. Dennis Hull put the Hawks back into the series in game three, leading his squad to a 7-4 revenge. Game four was highlighted by the netminding of Ken Dryden. He stopped every shot, while the Canadiens scored four on 'Tony O.' Game five was one of the most wide open encounters in modern Stanley Cup history. The teams combined for eight goals in the second period alone, and when referee Bruce Hood counted up the used pucks at game's end Chicago had eight to Montreal's seven. The teams continued firing the pill in game six. The score was tied at fours heading into the third period. Yvon Cournoyer blasted the winner and set up the insurance goal to send the Stanley Cup back to Le Belle Province once again.

Yvon Cournoyer set a new record for goals in NHL Stanley Cup play (15) and was awarded the Conn Smythe Trophy as the MVP of the playoffs..

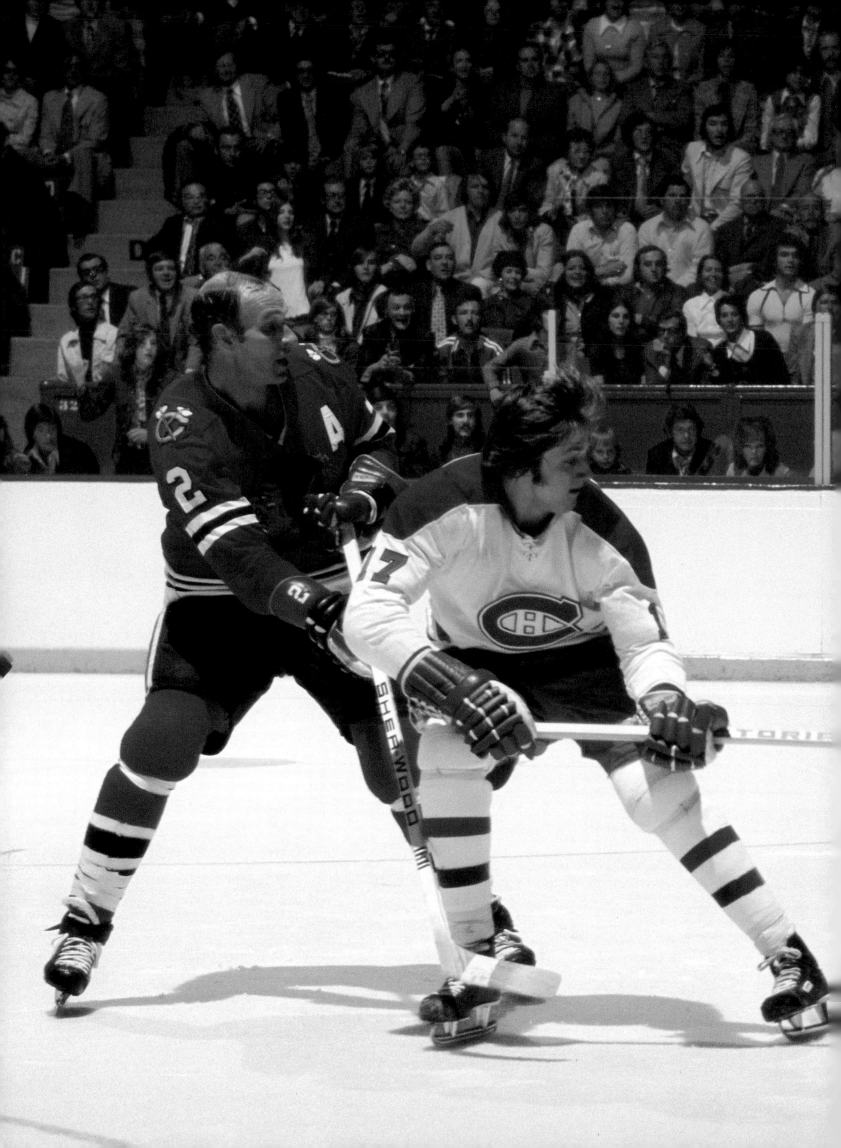

1974

Philadelphia vs Boston

The National Hockey League expanded into Georgia (Atlanta Flames) and added a second team to the New York area (New York Islanders) in this year. The Boston Bruins continued their presence at the high end of the NHL scale, gathering 52 wins and 113 points. They had the top four puck slingers in the league skating for their side – Phil Esposito, Bobby Orr, Ken Hodge and Wayne Cashman – who combined to score 180 goals in the season.

A new force was being felt in the West Division. The Philadelphia Flyers had progressed over the past seven years from a ragtag group of 'also-rans' to a formidable crew of seasoned National Leaguers. Their fans called them the Broad Street Bullies, and they earned the moniker by using tactics not seen in the major league since the 'alley bashing' Maple Leafs of the late 1940s.

It seemed inevitable that the two powerhouses of the NHL would meet in the Stanley Cup finals. In the early playoff rounds, the universe unfolded as predicted. After throwing aside the Maple Leafs and the Hawks, the Bruins were ready for the Flyers, who similarly dismissed the Atlanta Flames and the Rangers.

The first game of this memorable exchange was decided by Bobby Orr. Orr took a pass from Ken Hodge with just 22 seconds left in the game and slammed it past the stalwart Bernie Parent. Philadelphia lost the first game 3-2, but were determined to turn the tables on the Bears in this second game. The Flyers had not won a game in the Gardens in 19 tries. Boston scored two early goals, matched by the Flyers in the second and third periods, and the game was sent into overtime. Bill 'Cowboy' Flett lassoed a pass to Bobby Clarke and Captain Clarke drove it past a bewildered Gilles Gilbert to

1974

ABOVE: *Bobby Clarke (16) meshes with Carol Vadnais (10) for control of the puck, Cup finals, 1974.*

LEFT: *The Bruins celebrate a victory, a rare occurrence in the 1974 finals, as the Flyers went on to win the Cup in six games. Philadelphia won the Cup in only their seventh season, helped in large part by Bobby Clarke's overtime goal in game two, which halted a 19-game winless streak in Boston Garden for the Philadelphians.*

1974

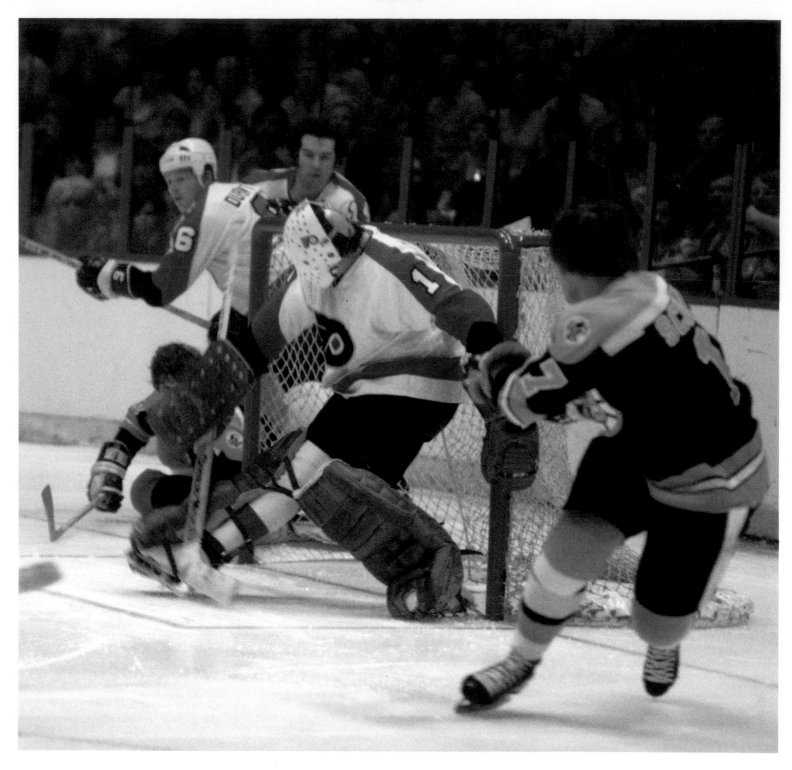

ABOVE: *Bernie Parent fires out his pad in rapier-like fashion to rob Bobby Schmautz (17), while Bobby Orr (4) awaits the rebound. Parent's heroics earned him the Conn Smythe Trophy.*

give the Flyers the Boston Garden win they would need to take the series. Buoyed by this victory, the Broad Street gang allowed one goal early in the first frame of game three, then answered with four of their own to pull ahead in the series.

Game four featured several first period donnybrooks, but the Flyers staggered out the victors courtesy of two third period goals by Bill Barber and Andre 'Moose' Dupont. This 4-2 Flyer triumph left them one game shy of the Stanley Cup. The Bruins came out fighting for their lives in game five. The match was interrupted

numerous times by fights of all sizes and descriptions, but when the teams left the ice Boston had pulled within one game of the Flyers. Game six was left in the capable hands of Bernie Parent. Rick MacLeish counted a power play goal in the first period and Parent took over shutting out the Bruins 1-0 and bringing the Stanley Cup to an unfamiliar resting place.

The Flyers became the first expansion club to win the Cup, and they thanked one man above the rest: Bernie Parent had been the heart of the team, and for his efforts, he was awarded the Conn Smythe Trophy.

1975

Philadelphia vs Buffalo

Another two teams made their debut in the NHL this season. The Kansas City Scouts and the Washington Capitals became the seventeenth and eighteenth franchises in the league. This led to the realignment of the league into the present-day format of two conferences (Wales and Campbell) and four divisions (Norris, Adams, Patrick and Smythe).

Bobby Orr returned to the top of the league scoring list, edging out teammate Phil Esposito for the honour. Two expansion teams led their divisions: The Buffalo Sabres, led by the 'French Connection' of Perreault, Martin, and Robert, won the Adams Division crown, while the Vancouver Canucks captured the Smythe. By the time the semifinal round began, only Buffalo would remain in the search for the 'Holy Grail.' The Sabres defeated the Montreal Canadiens in six games, and went on to play their first final round.

LEFT: *Buffalo goalie Gerry Desjardins lassoes 'Cowboy' Bill Flett, Buffalo vs. Philadelphia, 1975 finals.*

BELOW LEFT: *Rick Martin (7) and Ed Van Impe (2) do the tango Stanley Cup style, 1975.*

BELOW: *Rene Robert of the Sabres. The 1975 finals were the first to involve two expansion teams.*

1975

The New York Islanders became the first team since the 1942 Toronto Maple Leafs to come back from a three-game deficit to win their spot in the semifinal round. When they met the Flyers in the semi, they again came back after losing the first three games to tie the series, but lost a heartbreaking seventh game 4-1. The Philadelphia Flyers would meet the Buffalo Sabres in the first finals to feature two expansion clubs.

Philadelphia captured the first two games before the hometown fans, using a four goal third period to take the opener 4-1, and a third period power play goal to win the second match 2-1. Buffalo evened the match on their home ice, where Buffalo fans got their first taste of Stanley Cup fever. Rene Robert scored in overtime to give the Sabres a 5-4 win in game three, and the Sabres used this momentum to take the fourth game 4-2. Back on Broad Street, the Flyers exploded for five consecutive goals and waltzed past the Sabres 5-1 in the fifth game. There was no scoring in the sixth game until early in the third period. Bob 'Hound' Kelly scored only 11 seconds into the final frame and Bernie Parent shut out the Sabres 2-0, ruining the Cup dreams of the Buffalo faithful.

The Flyers had won back-to-back Stanley Cups, and Bernie Parent became the first and only man to win successive Conn Smythe trophies.

BELOW: *Winners and still champions: Bobby Clarke and Bernie Parent parade the Stanley Cup after game six of the 1975 finals, 27 May 1975. Parent became the first man to capture consecutive Conn Smythe trophies, recording four postseason 'zeros' and a microscopic 1.89 GAA in the 1975 postseason.*

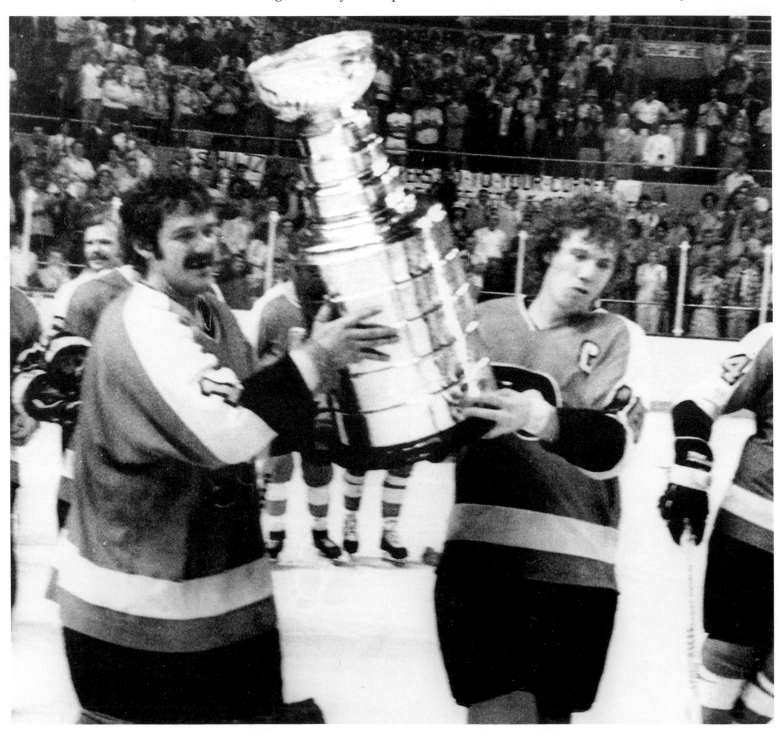

1976

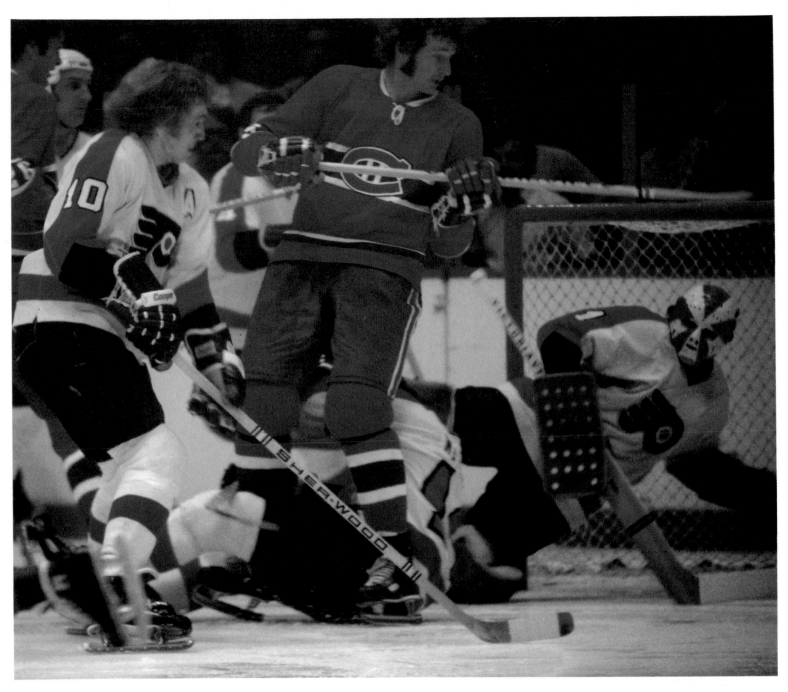

Montreal vs Boston

In 1971, Jean Beliveau had retired from the Montreal Canadiens, and the Habs had drafted Guy Lafleur in the hope that he might take up the torch held high by so many before him. Lafleur did not disappoint. In 1976, he topped the scoring race with 125 points, and helped to lead the Montreal Canadiens to a blockbuster season. The Habs finished 42 points ahead of their nearest rival in the Adams Division, and after knocking off Chicago and the New York Islanders reached the finals for the first time since 1973.

The Philadelphia Flyers were a picture of consistency, winning the Patrick Division crown and shoving aside Toronto and Bos-

ton to earn their third straight berth in the 'Silver Showdown.' Bob Clarke continued his outstanding play, finishing a close second to Guy Lafleur in the race for the Art Ross Trophy. His courage and determination exemplified the Flyer franchise and made him the favourite son of his adopted hometown.

The Flyers and Canadiens met in the Forum to decide this year's Stanley Cup ringbearers. The Canadiens spotted the Flyers an early 2-0 lead in game one but stormed back, scoring four goals to take the series lead. Guy Lafleur was the star of the second game, scoring an unassisted goal early in the third period to give Montreal a 2-1 victory and a two-game lead in the series. The Flyers fought back in game three,

ABOVE: *Malfunction at the junction: Larry Robinson (10) and Pete Mahovlich make life difficult for Bill Clement (10) and Flyer goalie Wayne Stephenson, Cup finals, 1976.*

but they could not control the explosive Montreal attack. Pierre Bouchard, whose father Butch Bouchard was a key member of the Montreal Canadiens of the 1950s, scored the game-winning goal in a 3-2 Montreal win. Game four once again belonged to Guy Lafleur. He scored the winning marker, set up by two others, and the Montreal Canadiens swept the Flyers in the Philadelphia Spectrum.

Reggie Leach set a new playoff record with 19 postseason goals. To mark the occasion, he was awarded the Conn Smythe Trophy. The Smythe generally is reserved for winning players, but Leach became the third player on a losing side to be given such an honour.

OPPOSITE: *Guy Lafleur, the Habs' hero.*

RIGHT: *Reggie Leach, Conn Smythe winner in a losing cause, 1976.*

BELOW: *Ken Dryden had a GAA of 1.92 in the 1976 playoffs.*

1977

Montreal vs Boston

The Montreal Canadiens of 1977 set team marks that may never be broken. They lost only eight games of an 80-game schedule, only one of these losses coming on home ice. They completely dominated the league, scoring 387 goals and allowing only 171. Guy Lafleur won the Art Ross Trophy and the Hart Trophy, and the Montreal Canadiens glided comfortably into the finals, losing only two of ten playoff games.

The competition to find a courageous suitor to meet this powerhouse was won by the Boston Bruins. The Bruins had neither Bobby Orr nor Phil Esposito in the lineup, but found strong replacements in Brad Park and Jean Ratelle. Boston skated into the finals, and like Montreal, had lost only two of ten playoff games.

TOP LEFT: *Jacques Lemaire's overtime goal in game four gave the Habs their second straight Cup victory.*

LEFT: *Guy Lafleur shows off his hardware, including the Conn Smythe, Art Ross and Hart trophies.*

ABOVE: *Don Marcotte (21) and Yvon Lambert (11).*

OPPOSITE: *Don Marcotte (21) lays the lumber on Bob Gainey (23).*

1977

ABOVE: *Terry O'Reilly (24) battles Guy Lapointe (5) in game three of the Cup finals, 12 May 1977.*

BELOW: *Celebrating Canadiens include Mario Tremblay (left) and Rejean Houle (right).*

The final series opened in Montreal, and the Habs' offence rekindled memories of the Flying Frenchmen of old. The lights were brighter than in those bygone days, but Guy Lafleur and Jacques Lemaire thrilled Forum fans with the speed and grace which has so long been associated with that ancient franchise. The Canadiens toyed with the Bruins in game one and celebrated a 7-3 victory. Game two featured shutout goaltending by Ken Dryden, and the Habs headed to Beantown two games up in the series, following a 3-0 decision. The Frenchmen were flying in game three, opening up an early three-goal lead and holding on to take the match 4-2. Boston fans were hungry for a win, but there would be no beans served at the Stanley Cup feast this year. Jacques Lemaire scored early in overtime to give the Montreal Canadiens the sweep of the series, and their eighteenth Stanley Cup parade.

Guy Lafleur added another notch to his award belt by winning the Conn Smythe Trophy.

1978

Montreal vs Boston

The Montreal Canadiens proved their 1977 season to have been no fluke, and this time lost only ten in their 80-game schedule. They stood head and shoulders above the rest of the league, and seemed destined, if there was any justice, to win yet another Stanley Cup.

The New York Islanders, in their fifth NHL season, made remarkable progress and finished with 111 points to win the Patrick Division. Bryan Trottier finished second in the scoring race and the Islanders were confident that they could unseat the mighty Habs. The Islander express was derailed, however, when they lost a gruelling seven-game series to the Toronto Maple Leafs. This set up a semifinal match between the Habs and the Leafs, the first time these two teams had met in postseason play since the infamous 1967 playoffs. The Canadiens were far too powerful for the young Leafs and raked them aside in four quick games.

BELOW: *Brian Engblom (3) slows down the pesky Terry O'Reilly (24). O'Reilly's fiery nature and Irish monicker made him a fan favourite in Beantown, but in the 1978 playoffs he showed an offensive spark as well, scoring 15 'second season' points.*

1978

The Boston Bruins also had an outstanding season and, after defeating Chicago and Philadelphia, made their way to the Forum in Montreal to face the Canadiens for the second consecutive Habs-Bruins final. Montreal continued where they had left off in 1977, taking both ends of their home stand by 4-1 and 3-2 scores. Boston fought back in the comfortable confines of Boston Garden. Gerry Cheevers shut out the Habs 4-0 in game three and Bobby Schmautz redirected a Brad Park shot past Ken Dryden in overtime to win game four by a 4-3 count. The Canadiens came out fast and hard in game five, scoring four consecutive goals in a 4-1 conquest. Montreal fulfilled their destiny in game six. Mario Tremblay put the Bears into hibernation with a brace of goals as the Canadiens won their third straight Cup in convincing fashion by a count of 4-1.

Larry Robinson had a standout postseason patrolling the blueline for the Canadiens. He scored four goals and led all playoff performers with 17 assists. His efforts were acknowledged by the Professional Hockey Writers Association, who selected him as the 1978 Conn Smythe Trophy winner.

OPPOSITE: *Larry Robinson tied for the 1978 playoff scoring lead and won the Conn Smythe Trophy.*

ABOVE: *Bobby Schmautz (11) is surrounded by teammates after scoring the overtime winner in game four of the Cup finals in 1978.*

BELOW: *Guy Lapointe (5) and Ken Hodge (9). Lapointe anchored the Canadiens' defence as the Habs won four consecutive Cups from 1976 to 1979.*

1979

Montreal vs N.Y. Rangers

The New York Islanders continued their re-markable progression, finishing first overall in the NHL with 116 points. The Isles were led by the 'Dynamic Duo' of Bryan Trottier, who led the league in points, and Mike Bossy, who scored more goals than any other National Leaguer. The Islanders were odds-on favourites for the finals this year, as they were in 1978, but they encountered a stubborn crosstown rival Ranger team who stopped them short in the semifinal round.

The Montreal Canadiens headed the class in the Norris Division, and their 115 points put them just one point behind the Isles for the NHL title. The Canadiens were well on their way to their fourth consecutive final appearance, having disposed of the Toronto Maple Leafs in four straight. The Canadiens met the Bruins in the semifinals, and Boston appeared to be on its way to dethroning the mighty Habs. The series was tied at three games apiece and Boston led 4-3 with only seconds left to play. In a now-infamous in-cident, the Bruins were called for too many men on the ice, and Montreal tied the score on the ensuing power play. Coach Don Cherry was a furious man without a Cup when, nine minutes later, Montreal packed up to head into the finals and the Bruins packed up for the season.

ABOVE: *Walt Tkaczuk (1) and Jacques Lemaire (25) are a study in concentration as they cross sticks in the face-off circle.*

LEFT: *Jacques Lemaire (25) led all scorers in goals (11) and total points (23) during the 1979 playoffs. Lemaire shocked all of Montreal the following season when he left the NHL to coach and play in Europe.*

1979

The New York Rangers met the Montreal Canadiens for the first time in a Stanley Cup final. The series opened in Montreal, where the New Yorkers shocked the Montreal faithful by outscoring the Habitants 4-1 and taking an important series lead. The Rangers jumped onto the scoreboard first in game two and held a 2-0 lead after just six minutes of play. Guy Lafleur got those two back in short order and Bob Gainey scored

the eventual game winner before the first intermission. On the heels of this 6-3 win, the Canadiens headed to Gotham City, where Montreal dominated the play and took the Rangers 4-1 in game three and 4-3 in overtime in the fourth tilt. The Canadiens came home anxious to finish off the Rangers on home ice. They had not won a Cup at home since 1968. In most NHL cities not winning Cups at home is the least of con-

BELOW: *Yvon Lambert (11) and Mario Tremblay celebrate as Canadien Ron Duguay skates unhappily away after Tremblay's key third period marker in game three of the Cup finals, 17 May 1979.*

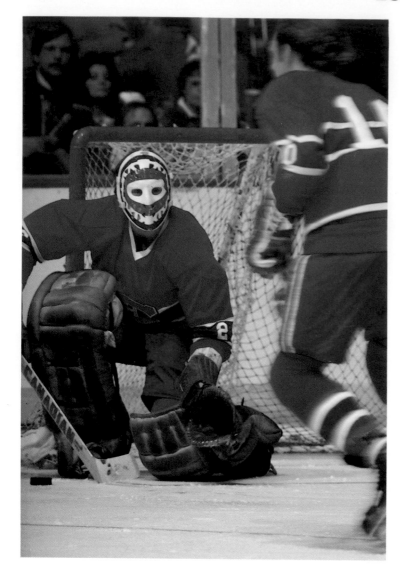

ABOVE: *Guy Lafleur (10) and Ken Dryden were the key components in the Montreal dynasty of the 1970s.*

ABOVE RIGHT: *Pierre Larouche wheels away from Phil Esposito (77) and Mike McEwen (27), Cup finals, 1979.*

RIGHT: *Bob Gainey (23) hoists the Cup after the Canadiens defeated the Rangers 4-1 in game five, 21 May 1979. Gainey, though not an offensive hero, was the true emotional leader of the Habs. His competitive spirit was rewarded when he won the 1979 Conn Smythe Trophy.*

cerns. The Canadiens, however, had been measured for no less than six sets of Stanley Cup rings in the ensuing 11 years, and winning at home would be the icing on the cake. The Habs spotted the Rangers an early one-goal lead, then roared back with four of their own and won the series and the game by the count of 4-1.

Bob Gainey, a consummate team player, is best known for his defensive skill, but in this series he tallied a number of important goals as well as being a focal point in all the games. It is this kind of play that gets a man's name engraved on the Conn Smythe Trophy.

The Canadiens had won their fourth straight Stanley Cup. On the way to winning them, they won 16 of 19 final series games to eliminate the competition. The Habs were on the way to matching the record they set in the 1950s, when they took five Stanley Cups in succession. The Montreal Canadiens, first formed in 1910, had gone on to become the winningest team in all of professional sports.

N.Y. Islanders vs Philadelphia

A treaty had been signed between the two professional hockey leagues which had been battling it out in the boardrooms and at the box office for the past seven years. The WHA went out of business, and four of their clubs entered the NHL. The Hartford Whalers, Winnipeg Jets, Edmonton Oilers, and Quebec Nordiques amalgamated with the NHL schedule, making the NHL 21 teams strong.

The playoff format had been revised, and now featured a system whereby 16 clubs would make the playoffs, and the best teams would play the worst teams in a series of encounters which would lead to an eventual Stanley Cup climax. The Philadelphia Flyers were the number one team in the league this year, followed by Montreal, Buffalo, and Boston. Marcel Dionne, now the 'old man of the sea' in Los Angeles, beat out the new 'wonderkin' Wayne Gretzky. Although they both registered 137 points, Dionne had scored two more goals than had Gretzky.

The New York Islanders saved the best for last this year, and after swamping L.A., Boston, and Buffalo, reached the elusive final round of Stanley Cup play. Montreal saw their quest stopped short when the Minnesota North Stars shocked all of Quebec, taking out the Habs in a seven-game marathon. The North Stars ran in to the Boys from Broad Street, who thrashed them in five uneven games. The Islanders were to meet the Flyers in the second Cup series to feature expansion clubs.

ABOVE: *Bob Nystrom (23), here in the clutches of Andre Dupont, was 'Mr. Clutch' for the Islanders, scoring numerous key goals for the Isles as they won their first Cup, in 1980. Nystrom and Billy Smith were the only 'original' Islanders left on the team that was formed in 1972.*

1980

RIGHT: *Bryan Trottier (19) and Bobby Clarke (16). Trottier was the leading scorer in the 1980 playoffs, winning the Conn Smythe Trophy.*

BELOW: *John Paddock (left) celebrates with Rick MacLeish after scoring in game six of the Cup finals, 24 May 1980.*

OPPOSITE TOP: *Bob Nystrom scores in the third period, helping the Isles to a 5-2 victory, 19 May 1980.*

OPPOSITE BOTTOM: *Bob Nystrom has just delivered the overtime goal that won the Cup for the Islanders, 24 May 1980. Nystrom's goal was the fourth overtime winner of his career.*

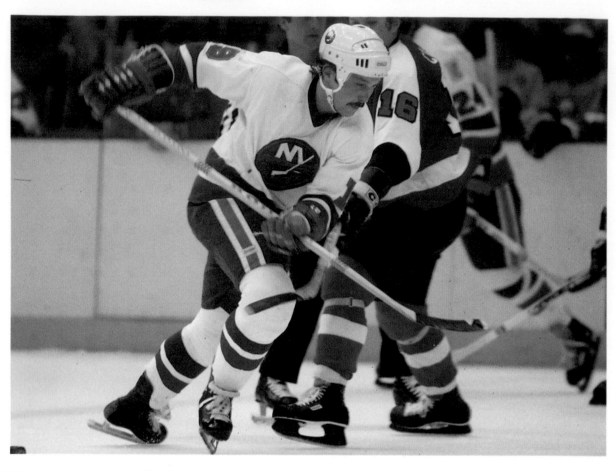

The Islanders used a three-point performance by Dennis Potvin, including the overtime winner, to take the edge in the first game 4-3. Philadelphia stormed back, firing eight pucks past the Islander netminders to win the second match 8-3. When the teams returned to Long Island, the hometown side exploded with six straight goals and skated off with a 6-2 win. The Islanders put themselves one slim win away from the Stanley Cup in game four. Clark Gillies scored one goal, set up a couple more, and the Islanders chalked up a 5-2 decision at the end of a hard night's work.

Philadelphia avoided elimination in game five, scoring a trio of goals in the second and third periods. With a 6-3 win under their belts, they headed back to the Nassau Coliseum. The teams traded goals in the first period, but the Islanders jumped ahead 4-2 after the second intermission. The Flyers evened up the tally in the third period, and the teams were tied heading into sudden death overtime. Seven minutes in, Bob Nystrom drove to the net and deflected a pass from John Tonelli past Pete Peeters, and the Stanley Cup returned to New York for the first time since 1940.

Bryan Trottier of the Isles led all playoff scorers in goals and total points, and was awarded the Conn Smythe Trophy.

1981

RIGHT: *Ken Morrow (6), a pain in the neck to the North Stars throughout the 1981 Cup finals, puts the hook on Al MacAdam. Minnesota's appearance in the 1981 finals was their first, and so far only, trip to Lord Stanley's feast.*

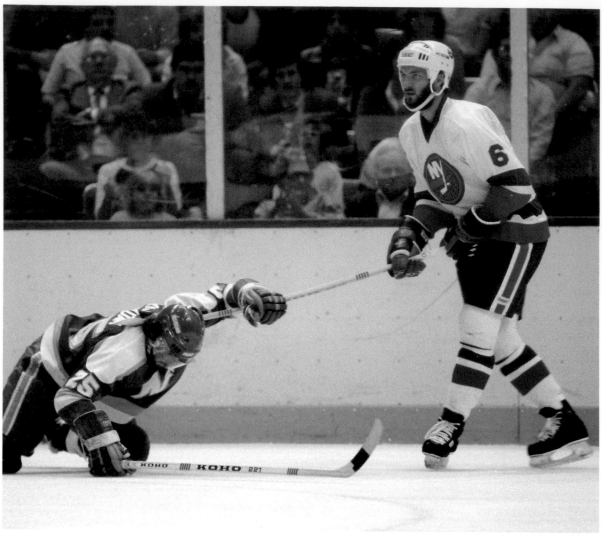

BELOW RIGHT: *Clark Gillies (9) runs some interference in front of Minnesota goalie Don Beaupre, 21 May 1981. Fred Barrett is the defender assigned to clear big Clark out of there.*

N.Y. Islanders vs Minnesota

The story of the 1981 season is the story of two men: Mike Bossy and Wayne Gretzky. The New York Islanders' Bossy reached a plateau which had been considered unattainable. In March, against the Quebec Nordiques, he fired a wrist shot which gave him 50 goals in 50 games, equalling the mark set by Maurice Richard in 1945. Wayne Gretzky, in his second NHL season, recorded a new high water mark by assisting on 109 goals, breaking Bobby Orr's 1971 record of 102.

The New York Islanders won the NHL season crown for the second consecutive time and after defeating the Leafs, Oilers, and Rangers in preliminary playoff rounds, reached the finals ready to defend their Silver Mug. The Minnesota North Stars, who finished third in the Adams Division, peaked at playoff time, defeating Boston, Buffalo, and Calgary to reach a pinnacle in their 13-year history. They prepared to meet the Islanders in their first Stanley Cup final.

The final set opened on Long Island and

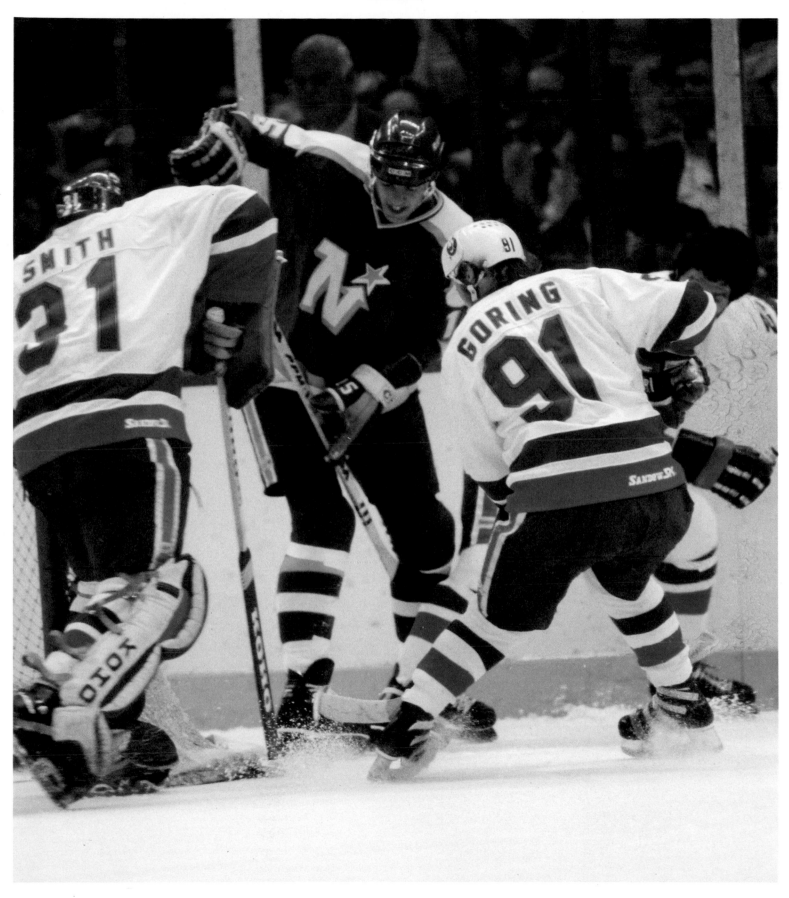

before the North Stars could shake the pre-game jitters, the Isles had a 4-0 lead. The Stars would get three back, but still wind up on the losing end of a 6-3 count. The youthful Minnesota squad, fronted by Bobby Smith and Steve Payne and backed by Gilles Meloche and Craig Hartsburg, came out strong in game two, opening the scoring in the first three minutes. The Islanders turned on the jets and propelled by Mike Bossy and Butch Goring, turned back the Stars by the same 6-3 result.

ABOVE: *Feisty Billy Smith and Butch Goring (91) gang up on Bobby Smith, Cup finals, 1981.*

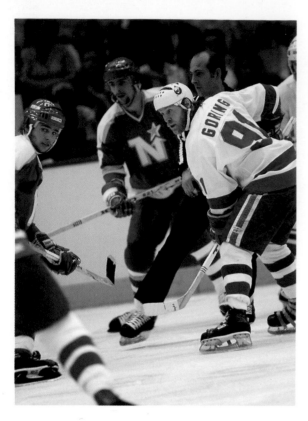

ABOVE: *Butch Goring's determination was rewarded when he received the Conn Smythe Trophy in 1981.*

RIGHT: *Bobby Smith (15) was the offensive sparkplug for the North Stars in the 1981 finals.*

The teams journeyed to Bloomington, Minnesota, where Minnesota fans got their first taste of Stanley Cup sharpshooting. The Stars again started out strong and at the end of the first period held a 3-0 lead. The balance of the contest belonged to the New Yorkers. They outscored the Stars 6-2 over the final two frames, winding up 7-5 victors. In game four, Minnesota used a balanced attack by shooters Steve Payne and Bobby Smith to stave off elimination and forced a fifth game on the Island with a 4-2 win. The Islanders could taste Stanley Cup champagne and, after Butch Goring's second goal, had an early 3-0 lead. They held off the Stars and when the final whistle blew, the Isles had a 5-1 victory and a second skate on the Stanley Cup pond.

Butch Goring's name indicates the kind of player he is. He plays a rough, tough, dog-eat-dog style of game, earning the respect of friend and foe alike. Despite his 5ft 9in and 160-pound stature, this centerman has never been afraid to carry the puck over the line. His determination and his rapid-fire wrist shot this year earned him the Conn Smythe Trophy.

ABOVE: *Islanders vs. Canucks, game one, 8 May 1982.*

OPPOSITE: *Denis Potvin (left) and Darcy Rota, Cup finals, 1982.*

BELOW: *Mike Bossy, Conn Smythe winner, 1982.*

N.Y. Islanders vs Vancouver

Wayne Gretzky really got started on his autobiography this season. He calls it *The NHL Record Book*, and it starts with his scoring 50 goals in 39 games. By the time his season was over, he had found the bull's-eye not less than 92 times, demolishing the records for goals (92), assists (120), points (212) and hat tricks (10). The most valued prize eluded his grasp, however, and his Oilers were eliminated by the lowly Los Angeles Kings in a shocking upset during the preliminary round of postseason play.

The New York Islanders were once again the class of the NHL. Billy Smith won the Vezina Trophy, Mike Bossy finished second in the scoring race, and Bryan Trottier reached the 50-goal plateau for the first time in his NHL career. After surviving a scare against the Pittsburgh Penguins in the first round, they walked over the Rangers and the Nordiques to secure their defence for the third time.

Los Angeles' dramatic victory over Edmonton could not carry them past a determined Vancouver squad. The Canucks took out Chicago in the semifinals and rolled into the finals for their first trip up the Stanley Cup canal. The Canucks had no superstars, but relied on the goaltending of 'King' Richard Brodeur, the scoring of Thomas Gradin and the leadership of Tiger Williams.

The series opened on Long Island and the Canucks battled the Islanders goal for goal

1982

LEFT: *The Islanders (left to right: Langevin, Tonelli, Persson and Nystrom) celebrate a goal in game two of the Cup finals in 1982. The Islanders eased past the Canucks in a four-game sweep to win their second Stanley Cup. Vancouver's march into the finals was helped by the L.A. Kings, who knocked off the favoured Edmonton Oilers in a quarter-final shocker. The Canucks then ripped both L.A. and Chicago to reach the ultimate test, the Stanley Cup finals.*

RIGHT: *Bob Nystrom puts the nail in the Canucks' coffin in game three, 13 May 1982, by scoring this empty netter in the Islanders' 3-0 victory.*

through 60 minutes of tenacious competition. The teams battled through overtime when, with just two seconds remaining in the first overtime, Mike Bossy stole the pill and delivered a prescription of his own for 'OT' hockey. Bossy's dramatics gave the Islanders a 6-5 triumph and the series lead. The Canucks fought back in game two and held a 3-2 lead entering the final 20 minutes. Ron Wicks had barely dropped the puck when Bob Bourne tied the score and when the frame ended, the Canucks had dropped a 6-4 decision to the Islanders.

The Pacific Coliseum crowd came to the rink equipped for the showers. They waved white towels of every description whenever the officials called against the hometown side. In an earlier match, several calls were questioned by coach Roger Neilson who waved such a towel to the referee, marking his surrender under unbeatable odds. Tonight it was white towels for Vancouver. They were going to need them. The Islanders' Gillies, Bossy and Nystrom delivered unrequited bull's-eyes, leaving the Isles one win shy of their third Stanley Cup. The crowd returned three days later with their now damp and salty towels at the ready. The teams were deadlocked at the end of the first period, but Mike Bossy took advantage of two power play situations, and put the game out of reach of the Canucks. When the shooting was over, the Islanders had won the game 3-1 and with it their third Stanley Cup.

Mike Bossy, who led all playoff scorers with 17 goals, was awarded the Conn Smythe Trophy.

1983

N.Y. Islanders vs Edmonton

Despite Wayne Gretzky's 'slump' (he would end up with only 196 points this year) the Edmonton Oilers still won the Smythe Division, finishing tied for second in the overall NHL standings. The Oilers would not relive the embarrassment of the 1982 postseason. They steamrolled into the finals having won 11 games and losing only one.

The Islanders finished second to the Philadelphia Flyers in the Patrick Division. They kept their hopes alive for a fourth straight shot at the Silver by defeating Washington, the New York Rangers, and the league-leading Boston Bruins.

There was great anticipation for this battle of the titans. The Oilers had scored an overwhelming 424 goals in the regular season, and the Islanders had allowed the fewest goals, 226. The series opened at the Northlands Coliseum in Edmonton and it was the Islander defensive unit that controlled this match. Duane Sutter scored an early first period goal and Ken Morrow added an empty netter as the Islanders shut out the powerful Oiler attack squad 2-0.

The Oilers scored first in game two, Dave Semenko giving them the early lead. The Islanders, however, stormed back smoking six of their own past a rattled Andy Moog and, on the heels of a 6-3 win, headed back to the Island for game three. The two squads traded goals in the first two frames and

1983

1983

BELOW: Billy Smith, who allowed only six goals in the 1983 finals, added the 1983 Conn Smythe Trophy to his collection.

headed into the third tied at ones. The Isles fired four consecutive markers and captured the third game by a 5-1 count. The Islanders were not about to let this band of Alberta puckslingers spoil their sweep. The New Yorkers scored three goals in a one-minute-and-thirty-second span of the first period, and cruised into the winner's circle with a 4-2 win.

The New York Islanders had equalled the mark of the Montreal Canadiens of the 1970s by winning four consecutive Stanley Cups and 16 of 19 final round games over the four-year span. However, this would prove to be the last great victory of the Islanders' dynasty. Billy Smith, the Jennings Trophy winner during the regular campaign, added the 1983 Conn Smythe Trophy to his collection.

1984

Edmonton vs N.Y. Islanders

The Great One, Wayne Gretzky, surpassed the 200-point mark again this season, and his Edmonton Oilers won the overall NHL title for the first time in their history. Paul Coffey finished second in the scoring race, the first time since Bobby Orr that a defence-man finished that high in the standings.

The New York Islanders captured the Patrick Division pennant for the fifth time in their history and after downing the Rangers, Washington and Montreal, reached the Stanley Cup final for the fifth year in a row. They stood poised to equal a record many thought would never be broken: the Montreal Canadiens' record of five straight Stanley Cup wins.

The Oilers cruised past Winnipeg, defeated Calgary in a hard seven-game series, then swept Minnesota to arrive at the final round for the second straight year.

The finals began in New York, where the Oilers gave notice they would be putting up a tougher struggle this year than they had in the 1983 sweep. The first game was score-

less through the first two periods, but Kevin McClelland gave the Oilers a 1-0 lead early in the third frame. Edmonton then put up a defensive wall around goaltender Grant Fuhr and made this one-goal lead stick,

1984

ABOVE: *Even the New York fans couldn't light a fire under the Islanders: Cup finals, 1984.*

taking the series lead. The Islanders came out firing in game two, scoring at the 53-second mark and adding three power play goals to skate away with a 6-1 victory. The teams returned to Edmonton where the Islanders held a 2-1 lead early in the second period. From that point forth it was all Edmonton. They blasted six unanswered goals, cutting through the New York defence at will. Mark Messier had a brace and Wayne Gretzky had a pair of helpers as the Oilers thrashed the Islanders 7-2. It was the same story in the fourth game. Messier and Gretzky each scored unassisted goals, pulling the Oilers within one game of the

Stanley Cup with another 7-2 triumph. In game five, Jari Kurri set up Number 99 for a pair of first period markers, then potted a power play goal of his own in the second, helping the Oilers spoil the dreams of the Isles by a score of 5-2. Although pro hockey has a long and admirable history in Edmonton, the Oilers would be the first Edmonton team to bring the Stanley Cup home.

A determined and highly skilled hockey player, Mark Messier is a natural leader of men and a fierce competitor. This year he would be judged the Most Valuable Player in the playoffs and awarded the Conn Smythe Trophy.

1984

ABOVE: *Jari Kurri (17) has the upper hand on Bryan Trottier (19), Cup finals, 1984. The Oilers showed they could play a tough defensive style of hockey by shutting out the Islanders 1-0 in game one of the finals. The victory proved to the Oilers that they could match the four-time Cup winners in every department.*

LEFT: *(L-r) Greg Gilbert, Bryan Trottier and Paul Coffey, Cup finals, 1984.*

1985

RIGHT: *The Oilers' 'super fan' cheers the troops on, Cup finals, 1985. There would be plenty to cheer about as the Cup stayed in Alberta. The Edmonton faithful watched a dynasty being formed as the Oilers rolled through the postseason, losing only three games. The Oilers set a number of records during these playoffs: Wayne Gretzky set marks for assists (30) and points (47), while Jari Kurri tied a playoff milestone for goals with 19, including a record four hat tricks. Paul Coffey also reached the NHL record book with new high water marks for goals (12), assists (25), and points (37) by a defenceman.*

Edmonton vs Philadelphia

The Edmonton Oilers won the Smythe Division title and had three of the top NHL scoring leaders (Gretzky, Kurri and Coffey). The Philadelphia Flyers won the overall NHL title with help from 54-goal scorer Tim Kerr. Mario Lemieux was named Rookie of the Year, compiling 100 points to herald his arrival in the realm of the superstars.

The Oilers breezed past Los Angeles, Winnipeg, and Chicago to reach the Stanley Cup finals for the third time, while the Philadelphia Flyers swept the Rangers, then beat back the Islanders and the Nordiques to arrive in the final round.

The finals opened at the Spectrum in Philadelphia, and shortly after the strains of 'God Bless America' boomed through the building, the Flyers went to work. They carried a 1-0 lead into the third period before erupting for a trio of goals from the sticks of Sutter, Kerr, and Poulin. When the final whistle sounded, the Flyers had wrapped up a tidy 4-1 opening game present. Edmonton literally battled back in game two, beat-

LEFT: *Grant Fuhr's steady goaltending kept the Flyers grounded during the 1985 Cup finals, as the Oilers gushed to a five-game Cup win. In addition to playing every game for the Oilers in the playoffs, Fuhr put his name in the record book for another feat. He stopped two penalty shots in the finals, one from Ron Sutter and another off the stick of Dave Poulin. This marked the first time in Cup history that two shots were called in the finals, and the first time they were both stopped.*

ing the Flyers at their own rough style of play. After a penalty-filled second period, goals by Gretzky and Lindstrom had the Oilers ahead 2-1. David Hunter added an empty netter and the Oilers had evened the series at ones.

The rough stuff continued in game three, the first period featuring numerous roughing and high sticking infractions. Wayne Gretzky was at his best, scoring a first period hat trick and giving the Oilers a 3-0 lead. The Flyers fought back with two goals in the

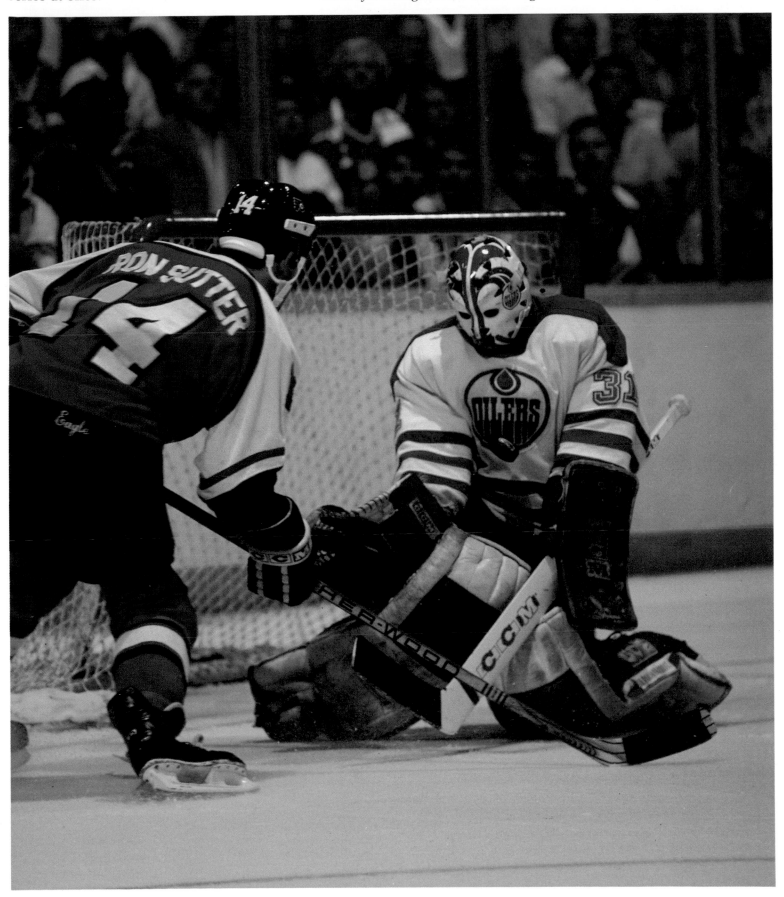

1985

third period, but still came up on the short end of a 4-3 score. Game four featured first period firepower, four of the five goals being scored by the specialty teams. The Flyers entered the second period leading 3-2, but once again Number 99 took control of the play. He scored a brace of goals, including the winner, and the Oilers stood one game away from the Cup, thanks to a 5-3 victory.

Edmonton wasted little time in game five. Led by Paul Coffey's two first period markers and Gretzky's pair in the second frame, they made babies out of the Broad Street Bullies, sending them back to the City of Brotherly Love with an 8-3 thrashing.

The Edmonton Oilers had won the Stanley Cup for the second time and in the doing, Wayne Gretzky earned the coveted Conn Smythe Trophy.

LEFT: *(L-r) Murray Craven, Jari Kurri and Wayne Gretzky, Cup finals, 1985.*   BELOW: *Derek Smith (24) is set upon by five Oilers but still manages to get a shot away, Cup finals, 1985.*

1986

LEFT: *The Montreal Canadiens converted plenty of these chances, but John Vanbiesbrouck, with help from Willie Huber (27) and James Patrick (3), foils this attempt by Bobby Smith (15) during the Cup semifinals, 7 May 1986. Montreal put the Rangers on the sidelines with a six-game triumph.*

BELOW: *Lanny McDonald (9) and Colin Patterson (11) combine to make life miserable for Montreal's Claude Lemieux. Lemieux scored two overtime goals in the 1986 playoffs, including the series winner against Hartford in game seven of the divisional semifinals.*

Montreal vs Calgary

Wayne Gretzky continued rewriting the NHL record book by setting new marks for assists (163) and total points (215). In fact, Gretzky had more assists than the second place finisher had total points. This outstanding individual performance helped his team win the NHL season title for a second time. The new kid on the block came calling this year: Mario Lemieux finished second in scoring with 141 points, but not enough to pull his Pittsburgh Penguins into the playoffs.

The Wales Conference playoffs featured a surprising performance by the Montreal Canadiens. The Habs swept by Boston and fought a determined Hartford squad to a seventh game, finally winning in overtime. Les Canadiens then ousted the New York Rangers to reach the Stanley Cup finals for the first time in this decade.

The Campbell Conference also had their share of surprises, none bigger than the Calgary Flames' dramatic seventh-game victory over the defending Oilers. Calgary, who had swept Winnipeg to reach the Edmonton series, had to fight another seven-game series with a very determined St. Louis Blues team. They again won the seventh game by a one-goal margin, and prepared to

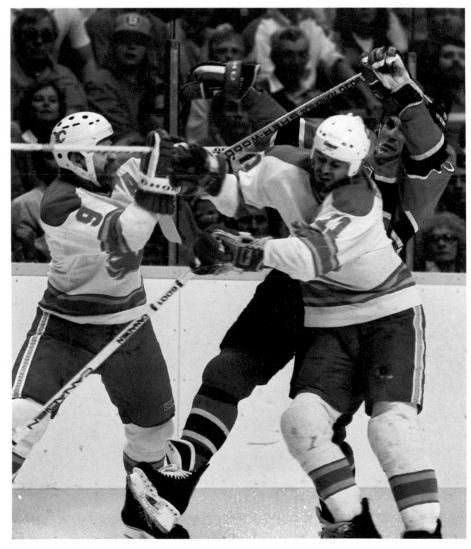

1986

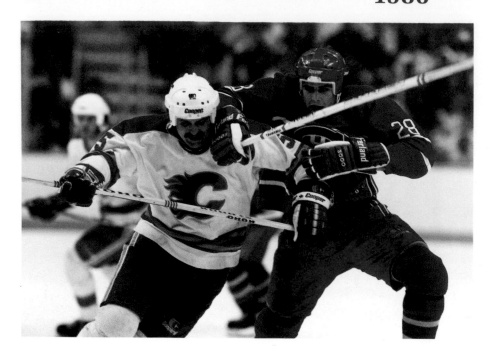

ABOVE: *Neil Sheehy (5) gets an unwanted massage from Montreal's Steve Rooney (28). Rooney only dressed for one game in the playoffs, but here he makes his presence felt, helping the Habs win their first Cup of the decade, 24 May 1986.*

the record book by scoring the fastest overtime goal in Stanley Cup history. Only nine seconds after referee Andy Van Hellemond faced the pill, Skrudland blasted one past Mike Vernon and the Canadiens had tied the series.

Game three was in the historic Montreal Forum. When Joel Otto scored Calgary's second power play goal of the first frame, they had a 2-1 lead with only two minutes remaining in the period. The Habs then exploded for three goals in one minute and eight seconds to erase Calgary's lead and take control of the game. Lanny McDonald added one more for the Flames, but it was not enough to beat the Habs on their home ice. Game four was a goaltenders' duel. The game remained scoreless until the midway point in the third period, when Claude Lemieux tallied the only marker the Habs would need on this night. Patrick Roy, the rookie goalie sensation, was at his absolute best, turning away all pretenders and shutting out the powerful Flames attack. The game was a rather tame affair until the final whistle sounded, when all hell broke loose. Eight players received game misconducts in one of the uglier scenes in modern Stanley Cup history.

The Habs were on their way to another Stanley Cup. It was a road they had been down before, but that didn't make it any

face off in their first Stanley Cup final.

Opening in Calgary, the Flames lit a fire under the Canadiens. Holding a 2-1 lead entering the third period, a brace of goals by Dan Quinn and Lanny McDonald in a one-minute span put the game on ice. With this 5-2 victory under their belts, the Flames readied themselves for game two. Calgary once again led 2-1 entering the third period of play, but a goal by David Maley tied the affair, sending the match into sudden death overtime. Bryan Skrudland put his name in

RIGHT: *Sheehy (5) gets a rough ride again, as Craig Ludwig puts the grip on him as they round the Habs' cage, Cup finals, 1986. Calgary, worn down by two seven-game series, against Edmonton and St. Louis, couldn't regain their momentum, losing the Cup to the Canadiens in five games.*
With the victory, Montreal set a new record for professional sports franchises, capturing their 23rd Stanley Cup. The Habs had been tied with the New York Yankees with 22 championships apiece.

easier. The Canadiens broke open a close match in the third period. Rick Greene and Bobby Smith scored 19 seconds apart to give the Habs a commanding 4-1 advantage. Calgary fought back with two more goals, but the spark fell short of catching ablaze, and with spirits doused, the Flames headed back to the prairies empty handed.

Patrick Roy, who brought back memories of another Canadiens' rookie sensation in the net, Ken Dryden, was awarded the Conn Smythe Trophy.

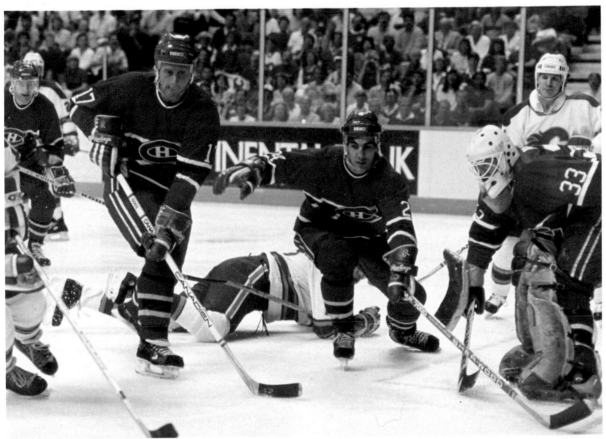

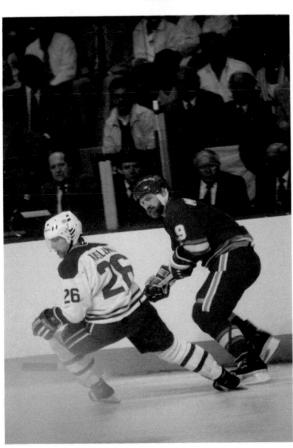

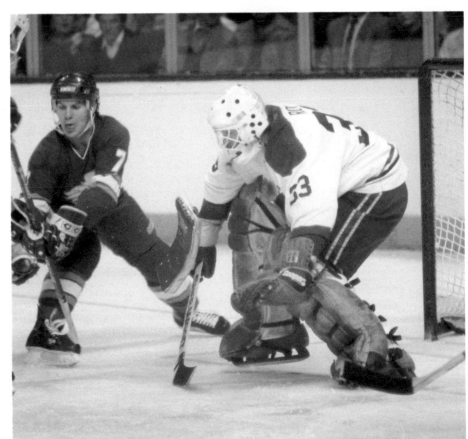

LEFT: *The Canadiens' defence of (l-r) Ludwig, Chelios and Roy combined to shut down the powerful Calgary offence. In addition to his defensive effort, Chelios gathered 11 points to lead all Montreal defencemen in playoff scoring.*

BELOW LEFT: *The Canadiens' five-game victory in 1986 left veteran Lanny McDonald (here being shadowed by Mats Naslund) still searching for his first Cup ring. McDonald scored 11 playoff goals, including four power play markers and one overtime winner.*

BELOW: *Patrick Roy's outstanding performance in the playoffs put the rookie's name on both the Stanley Cup and the 1986 Conn Smythe Trophy. Roy won 15 games while losing only five during the postseason showdown.*

1987

ABOVE: *Wayne Gretzky with part of his 1987 booty: the Stanley Cup, the Hart Trophy and the Lester B Pearson Award. The Pearson Award is given to the NHL's outstanding performer as selected by the players.*

RIGHT: *Dave Poulin (20) attempts to slow down Jari Kurri (17). The Oilers' speedy forward led all 1987 playoff scorers with 15 goals, including five game-winners.*

OPPOSITE: *The Greatest One: Wayne Gretzky led the Oilers to their third Cup in 1987, assisting on 29 goals and leading all playoff scorers with 34 points.*

Edmonton vs Philadelphia

The Edmonton Oilers continued their dominance of both the Smythe Division and the NHL scoring race. Wayne Gretzky, Jari Kurri, and Mark Messier all finished in the top four on the total-points leader board, and the Oilers were the number one team in the NHL. It was clear sailing for the Oilers and they set a course for the Stanley Cup finals. Edmonton downed L.A., Winnipeg, and Detroit, losing only two of 14 postseason matches.

The Philadelphia Flyers were once again the Patrick Division crown winners and they battled their way past the Rangers, the Islanders, and the defending champion Canadiens to reach their third Stanley Cup final of the decade.

The 17th of May marked the first game of the return match between the Oilers and Flyers, who had wrestled for Silver in 1985. The teams were tied entering the third period of game one, but a lightning-quick marker by Glenn Anderson and the eventual game winner by Paul Coffey put the Oilers ahead to stay, winning this first en-

counter 4-2. The Flyers held a 2-1 lead midway through the third period of game two. Glenn Anderson tied the affair, sending the game into sudden death overtime. Jari Kurri took a pass from Wayne Gretzky, and before the fourth period was seven minutes old he gave the Oilers a 3-2 victory. Back on Flyers' home ice the Oilers built an early 3-0 lead. Philadelphia fought back, and goals by Craven, Zezel, and Mellanby tied the game at threes. Just 17 seconds after Mellanby's marker, Brad McCrimmon fired the game winner and the Flyers brought the house to its feet with a 5-3 crowd pleaser. The Oilers pulled within one game of Stanley's Silver, foiling the Flyer defence and goalie Ron Hextall with a 4-1 triumph in game four.

Despite giving Edmonton an early 3-1 lead in game five, the determined Flyers regrouped and worked back to win the game 4-3. Brian Propp supplied the helpers on all four Flyer goals and was the clear offensive star of the game. In game six the Oilers, throwing their considerable weight around, pounced on the Philadelphia side for two quick goals. The third period saw the Flyers cheat death once again. Ron Hextall slammed the door on the Oiler attack squad and, led by goals by Propp and Daigneault only seconds apart, the Flyers deadlocked

1987

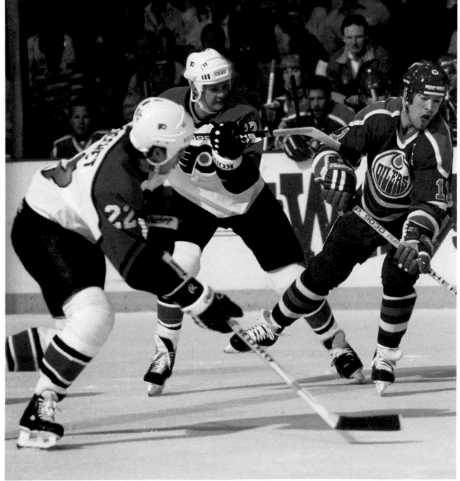

the series with a 3-2 thriller.

Game seven, the first such since 1971, was played before a wild hometown cheering section in Edmonton. Murray Craven opened the scoring for the Flyers, only to have Mark Messier even things up. With five minutes remaining in the second period, Jari Kurri converted a Wayne Gretzky pass, one-timing it past an oblivious Ron Hextall. Glenn Anderson added an insurance marker late in the third period, assuring there would be no more Flyer miracles. The Oilers returned to the winner's circle to receive their third Stanley Cup in four years.

Ron Hextall, whose storybook rise from the AHL to the NHL Stanley Cup finals won him the Conn Smythe Trophy, became the fourth player from a losing side to take home this award.

ABOVE: *Marty Howe (2) lets one fly while Messier (11) and Coffey (7) look on, Cup finals, 1987.*

LEFT: *Mark Messier controls the puck, Cup finals, 1987.*

1988

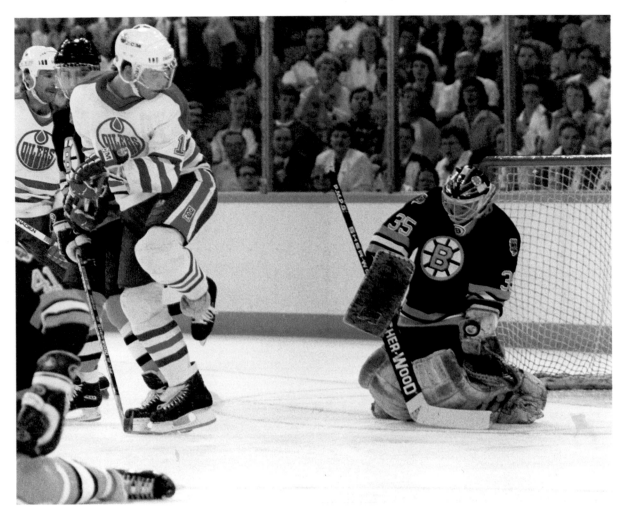

LEFT: *Andy Moog has a leg up on the Oilers' Craig Simpson as he smothers this shot during game one of the 1988 finals. The Oilers went on to win the series lid-lifter 2-1. Moog was a key member of three Oiler Cup-winning teams, but a contract dispute forced him to sit out a portion of the 1988 season. He was eventually traded to Boston and helped the Bruins reach the finals for the first time since 1978. He couldn't repeat his earlier Cup successes for the upstart Bruins, however. The Oilers put the Bears into hibernation by sweeping them out of the finals in four straight.*

Edmonton vs Boston

The 1988 season featured a number of firsts. The Calgary Flames won their first Smythe Division championship and their first NHL overall title. Detroit won their first Norris Division crown and the New Jersey Devils made it to the postseason for the first time since moving from Colorado. Perhaps the biggest news was that Wayne Gretzky's seven-year run as scoring leader and eight-year streak as Hart Trophy winner were both ended. Mario Lemieux took advantage of a Gretzky injury to lead the NHL in goals (70) and in total points (168). Despite his heroics, his Penguins would not fly into the playoffs.

The Wales Conference playoffs featured a number of outstanding playoff matches. New Jersey defeated the Islanders in six games and Washington in seven to reach the conference championship finals. It would take the Boston Bruins seven games to rid themselves of this pesky Devil team. This playoff round also supplied journalists with a field day. After berating referee Don Koharski following game three, Devil coach Jim Schoenfeld was suspended for one game. A New Jersey court overruled the sus-

pension, and Schoenfeld appeared behind the bench causing the on-ice officials to stage a walkout. Matters were resolved and the series continued without incident, Boston winning in seven games and entering the finals for the first time in ten years.

ABOVE: *Grant Fuhr proved himself to be the world's best between the pipes, winning both the 1988 Vezina and Conn Smythe trophies.*

1988

Calgary had great hopes of returning to the Stanley Cup finals, but these hopes were dashed by the Oilers. Edmonton swept Calgary, walked over Detroit, and entered their fourth final in five years, having lost only two postseason games.

The Bruins had their work cut out for them, and when the series opened in Edmonton their greatest fears began to take shape. In a closely contested first match the Oilers eked out a 2-1 victory, the winning marker being delivered by Keith Acton. The Bruins spotted the Oilers an early 2-0 lead in game two, but came back to tie on markers from Bob Joyce and Kenny Linseman. Wayne Gretzky shelved the Boston hopes, scoring the winning goal in a 4-2 Edmonton victory. The Oiler firepower continued in game three. They scored one in the first, two in the second, and three in the third to waltz past the Bears 6-3.

Game four provided one of the more unique stories in Stanley Cup lore. The Bruins, coming back from a 2-0 deficit, jumped into the lead when Glen Wesley scored his second of two goals. Craig Simpson drained one past former Oiler netminder Andy Moog at 16:37 of the second period. It was lights out for the Bruins; in fact it was lights out for everybody. A power failure at the exact moment in which Simpson's blast dented the twine caused the game to be suspended, to be completely replayed at the end of the series if needed. This marked the first time since 1951 that a playoff game could not be completed. Iron-

ically it was the Boston Bruins who participated in that match as well. Game four/five was played in Edmonton, where the Oilers canned the Beantowners and sent the Bears back to their cave to lick their wounds in a 6-3 Cup-clinching performance.

Wayne Gretzky became the third man to win the Conn Smythe Trophy twice, receiving this year's award for his new additions to the record book. He set marks for most points (13) and most assists (10) in this remarkable four-and-one-half game final series.

ABOVE: *Craig Simpson (18) goes for a spill thanks to a well-placed cross-check by Cam Neely (8) in game two of the 1988 finals. Simpson tallied 56 goals in 1988, 43 of them coming after his trade from Pittsburgh to Edmonton.*

BELOW: *Kevin McClelland (24) and Randy Burridge at close quarters during the 1988 finals. The Oilers used a well-balanced attack coupled with strong defence to win their fourth Cup in five years. Edmonton powered their way through the 1988 playoffs, winning 16 games while losing only two. Their appearance in the finals marked the sixth consecutive year a team from Alberta made it to the final battle for the 'Silver Mug.'*

1989

Calgary vs Montreal

In the summer of 1988, the hockey world was buzzing with rumours of a remarkable trade: Would Edmonton Oilers owner Peter Pocklington really let Wayne Gretzky go? Major stars always seem the least likely players to be traded, but in fact, history shows that most find themselves on the auction block at some point in their careers. So it was with Wayne Gretzky. In the fall of that year, the Great One went south to Los Angeles, to play for Kings owner Bruce McNall.

The Oilers would pay dearly for trading their captain within their own division, and Gretzky would come back to haunt them: The newly-crowned Kings eliminated the defending Cup champions in a thrilling seven-game series complete with a Hollywood ending, with Gretzky scoring an empty-net goal before the who's who of American entertainment in Los Angeles.

In the other divisions, the status quo remained intact. Montreal, who finished second to Calgary in the regular season, cruised past Hartford, Boston, and Philadelphia to reach their second Stanley Cup final of the 1980s. Their opponents in 1989 would be the same as in 1986. The Calgary Flames completed the 1989 season by winning their second consecutive President's Trophy, and were odds-on favourites to keep the Cup in Alberta. After surviving a score from a tenacious Vancouver Canuck team, they whitewashed Los Angeles, choked off Chicago and arrived at Stanley Cup center ice at last.

Game one in Calgary opened in uncharacteristic fashion, with four goals being scored in the opening ten minutes. Calgary pepper pot Theoren Fleury broke a 2-2 tie by firing a second-period shot between the legs of Patrick Roy to give the Flames a 3-2 victory. The Habs counterattacked in game two, and caught the red-eye back to Montreal tied at ones in the series after a 4-2 victory.

Calgary dominated much of game three, and with only a handful of ticks left on the clock had a 3-2 lead. Mats Naslund intercepted a Flames' clearing pass and fired a bullet into the top corner, setting the stage

BELOW: *The King and his Court: Wayne Gretzky battles his ex-teammate Jari Kurri in the Smythe Division semifinals. In a series unmatched for its emotional excitement the Kings, led by Number 99, defeated Edmonton in seven action-packed contests. The Kings were unable to find the same motivation in their next series, against Calgary, and succumbed to the eventual Stanley Cup champs in four straight games. However, by ousting the defending champion Oilers, the Kings had achieved a feat many thought would be impossible.*

1989

for the second longest overtime game in Stanley Cup history. Montreal fans hit the streets in a joyous mood after Ryan Walter flicked a shot from just outside the crease past Mike Vernon at the 38-minute mark in overtime, to give the Canadiens a 4-3 win. Game four was dominated by goaltending heroics and a player whose shot is known as the 'howitzer': Al MacInnis scored the winning goal and added an assist, and the Calgary Flames headed back out west with the series tied at two games apiece following their 4-2 triumph.

In game five the Flames moved one step closer to their first-ever Stanley Cup victory, throwing a defensive blanket around the weary Habs and skating them into the ice with a nail-biting 3-2 win thanks to a second-period goal by Al MacInnis. The teams returned to Montreal where, despite a 3-2 lead, the odds seemed to be stacked against the Flames. Montreal had never allowed an opposing team to win the Cup on Forum ice, and had not lost three games in a row all season long. Calgary's Lanny McDonald, a 16-year veteran, was not about to let tradition get in the way of his first Stanley Cup. His second-period goal gave the Flames a lead they would never relin-

quish, and when Doug Gilmour clipped the puck into the yawning cage, the Flames had closed the game and the series by a 4-2 count.

Al MacInnis set a playoff record by scoring at least one point in 17 consecutive games. This offensive display, coupled with his solid defensive work, earned him the Conn Smythe Trophy.

ABOVE: Al MacInnis tangles with Shane Corson, Cup finals, 1989. MacInnis won the Conn Smythe Trophy.

BELOW: Doug Gilmour (39) was a key factor in the Flames' 1989 Cup victory.

In 1991, the Stanley Cup will be due for a change. Following the final series that spring, there will be no more room on the cup for the names of its champions. The Cup may take on a new look — something that has certainly happened before.

When Lord Stanley donated the prize in 1893, the Cup was a bowl approximately 7½" in height. With each passing year, bands were added to its base until, in 1948, the NHL made a substantial change in the Cup's appearance. This version of the Cup was basically the same shape we see now, but the detail was far different. Below the collar, bands of uneven size boasted the names of the winning clubs. There seems to have been little control over how wide each band would be, or how many names would be put on the Cup. In 1957, the Cup took on its current look, with evenly-spaced bands

below the collar area. The winning club has 17 square inches in which to inscribe the many names they include in their championship roster. In 1970, a replacement was crafted for the original bowl. The alloys used in the 1893 silversmith shop had done their service, and the league retired the original to the Hockey Hall of Fame for permanent display.

There is speculation that the league would like to get one extra year of service out of the current Cup, bringing the trophy to its centennial year — an appropriate time to make substantial changes in its appearance.

What the Stanley Cup of the future will look like is anyone's guess. What we know for certain is that it will continue to serve as the raison d'etre for stick handling boys on backyard rinks across the entire northern hemisphere.

ABOVE: *A proud group of Calgary Flames poses with the ultimate prize in professional sport: the Stanley Cup, Cup finals, 1989.*

STANLEY CUP CHAMPIONS AND FINALISTS

YEAR	WINNING TEAM	WINNING COACH	LOSING TEAM	LOSING COACH
1989	Calgary Flames	Terry Crisp	Montreal Canadiens	Pat Burns
1988	Edmonton Oilers	Glen Sather	Boston Bruins	Terry O'Reilly
1987	Edmonton Oilers	Glen Sather	Philadelphia Flyers	Mike Keenan
1986	Montreal Canadiens	Jean Perron	Calgary Flames	Bob Johnson
1985	Edmonton Oilers	Glen Sather	Philadelphia Flyers	Mike Keenan
1984	Edmonton Oilers	Glen Sather	New York Islanders	Al Arbour
1983	New York Islanders	Al Arbour	Edmonton Oilers	Glen Sather
1982	New York Islanders	Al Arbour	Vancouver Canucks	Roger Neilson
1981	New York Islanders	Al Arbour	Minnesota North Stars	Glen Sonmor
1980	New York Islanders	Al Arbour	Philadelphia Flyers	Pat Quinn
1979	Montreal Canadiens	Scotty Bowman	New York Rangers	Fred Shero
1978	Montreal Canadiens	Scotty Bowman	Boston Bruins	Don Cherry
1977	Montreal Canadiens	Scotty Bowman	Boston Bruins	Don Cherry
1976	Montreal Canadiens	Scotty Bowman	Philadelphia Flyers	Fred Shero
1975	Philadelphia Flyers	Fred Shero	Buffalo Sabres	Floyd Smith
1974	Philadelphia Flyers	Fred Shero	Boston Bruins	Armand 'Bep' Guidolin
1973	Montreal Canadiens	Scotty Bowman	Chicago Black Hawks	Billy Reay
1972	Boston Bruins	Tom Johnson	New York Rangers	Emile Francis
1971	Montreal Canadiens	Al MacNeil	Chicago Black Hawks	Billy Reay
1970	Boston Bruins	Harry Sinden	St. Louis Blues	Scotty Bowman
1969	Montreal Canadiens	Claude Ruel	St. Louis Blues	Scotty Bowman
1968	Montreal Canadiens	Hector 'Toe' Blake	St. Louis Blues	Scotty Bowman
1967	Toronto Maple Leafs	George 'Punch' Imlach	Montreal Canadiens	Hector 'Toe' Blake
1966	Montreal Canadiens	Hector 'Toe' Blake	Detroit Red Wings	Sid Abel
1965	Montreal Canadiens	Hector 'Toe' Blake	Chicago Black Hawks	Billy Reay
1964	Toronto Maple Leafs	George 'Punch' Imlach	Detroit Red Wings	Sid Abel
1963	Toronto Maple Leafs	George 'Punch' Imlach	Detroit Red Wings	Sid Abel
1962	Toronto Maple Leafs	George 'Punch' Imlach	Chicago Black Hawks	Rudy Pilous
1961	Chicago Black Hawks	Rudy Pilous	Detroit Red Wings	Sid Abel
1960	Montreal Canadiens	Hector 'Toe' Blake	Toronto Maple Leafs	George 'Punch' Imlach
1959	Montreal Canadiens	Hector 'Toe' Blake	Toronto Maple Leafs	George 'Punch' Imlach
1958	Montreal Canadiens	Hector 'Toe' Blake	Boston Bruins	Milt Schmidt
1957	Montreal Canadiens	Hector 'Toe' Blake	Boston Bruins	Milt Schmidt
1956	Montreal Canadiens	Hector 'Toe' Blake	Detroit Red Wings	Jimmy Skinner
1955	Detroit Red Wings	Jimmy Skinner	Montreal Canadiens	Dick Irvin
1954	Detroit Red Wings	Tommy Ivan	Montreal Canadiens	Dick Irvin
1953	Montreal Canadiens	Dick Irvin	Boston Bruins	Lynn Patrick
1952	Detroit Red Wings	Tommy Ivan	Montreal Canadiens	Dick Irvin
1951	Toronto Maple Leafs	Joe Primeau	Montreal Canadiens	Dick Irvin
1950	Detroit Red Wings	Tommy Ivan	New York Rangers	Lynn Patrick
1949	Toronto Maple Leafs	Clarence 'Happy' Day	Detroit Red Wings	Tommy Ivan
1948	Toronto Maple Leafs	Clarence 'Happy' Day	Detroit Red Wings	Tommy Ivan
1947	Toronto Maple Leafs	Clarence 'Happy' Day	Montreal Canadiens	Dick Irvin
1946	Montreal Canadiens	Dick Irvin	Boston Bruins	Aubrey 'Dit' Clapper
1945	Toronto Maple Leafs	Clarence 'Happy' Day	Detroit Red Wings	Jack Adams
1944	Montreal Canadiens	Dick Irvin	Chicago Black Hawks	Paul Thompson
1943	Detroit Red Wings	Jack Adams	Boston Bruins	Art Ross
1942	Toronto Maple Leafs	Clarence 'Happy' Day	Detroit Red Wings	Jack Adams
1941	Boston Bruins	Ralph 'Cooney' Weiland	Detroit Red Wings	Ebbie Goodfellow
1940	New York Rangers	Frank Boucher	Toronto Maple Leafs	Dick Irvin
1939	Boston Bruins	Art Ross	Toronto Maple Leafs	Dick Irvin
1938	Chicago Black Hawks	Bill Stewart	Toronto Maple Leafs	Dick Irvin
1937	Detroit Red Wings	Jack Adams	New York Rangers	Lester Patrick
1936	Detroit Red Wings	Jack Adams	Toronto Maple Leafs	Dick Irvin
1935	Montreal Maroons	Tommy Gorman	Toronto Maple Leafs	Dick Irvin
1934	Chicago Black Hawks	Tommy Gorman	Detroit Red Wings	Herbie Lewis
1933	New York Rangers	Lester Patrick	Toronto Maple Leafs	Dick Irvin
1932	Toronto Maple Leafs	Dick Irvin	New York Rangers	Lester Patrick
1931	Montreal Canadiens	Cecil Hart	Chicago Black Hawks	Dick Irvin
1930	Montreal Canadiens	Cecil Hart	Boston Bruins	Art Ross
1929	Boston Bruins	Cy Denneny	New York Rangers	Lester Patrick
1928	New York Rangers	Lester Patrick	Montreal Maroons	Eddie Gerard
1927	Ottawa Senators	Dave Gill	Boston Bruins	Art Ross

(The National Hockey League took over sole control of Stanley Cup competition after 1926)

YEAR	WINNING TEAM	WINNING COACH	LOSING TEAM	LOSING COACH
1926	Montreal Maroons	Eddie Gerard	Victoria Cougars	Lester Patrick
1925	Victoria Cougars	Lester Patrick	Montreal Canadiens	Leo Dandurand
1924	Montreal Canadiens	Leo Dandurand	Calgary Tigers	—
			Vancouver Maroons	—
1923	Ottawa Senators	Pete Green	Edmonton Eskimos	—
			Vancouver Maroons	—
1922	Toronto St. Pats	Eddie Powers	Vancouver Millionaires	Frank Patrick
1921	Ottawa Senators	Pete Green	Vancouver Millionaires	Frank Patrick

Year	Winner	Coach	Challenger	Coach
1920	Ottawa Senators	Pete Green	Seattle Metropolitans	–
1919	No decision (series between Montreal and Seattle called off due to influenza epidemic)			
1918	Toronto Arenas	Dick Carroll	Vancouver Millionaires	Frank Patrick
1917	Seattle Metropolitans	–	Montreal Canadiens	–
1916	Montreal Canadiens	–	Portland Rosebuds	–
1915	Vancouver Millionaires	–	Ottawa Senators	–
1914	Toronto Blueshirts	–	Victoria Cougars	–
			Montreal Canadiens	–
1913	Quebec Bulldogs	–	Sydney Miners	–
1912	Quebec Bulldogs	–	Moncton Victorias	–
1911	Ottawa Senators	–	Port Arthur Bearcats	–
			Galt	–
1910	Montreal Wanderers	–	Berlin Union Jacks	–
			Edmonton Eskimos	–
			Galt	–
1909	Ottawa Senators	–	(no challengers)	
1908	Montreal Wanderers	–	Edmonton Eskimos	–
			Toronto Trol. Leaguers	–
			Winnipeg Maple Leafs	–
			Ottawa Victorias	–
1907	Montreal Wanderers	–	Kenora Thistles	–
	Kenora Thistles	–	Montreal Wanderers	–
1906	Montreal Wanderers	–	New Glasgow Cubs	–
			Ottawa Silver Seven	–
	Ottawa Silver Seven	–	Montreal Wanderers	–
			Smith's Falls	–
			Queens University	–
1905	Ottawa Silver Seven	–	Rat Portage Thistles	–
			Dawson City Nuggets	–
1904	Ottawa Silver Seven	–	Brandon Wheat Kings	–
			Montreal Wanderers	–
			Toronto Marlboros	–
			Winnipeg Rowing Club	–
1903	Ottawa Silver Seven	–	Rat Portage Thistles	–
			Montreal Victorias	
	Montreal AAA	–	Winnipeg Victorias	–
1902	Montreal AAA	–	Winnipeg Victorias	–
	Winnipeg Victorias	–	Toronto Wellingtons	–
1901	Winnipeg Victorias	–	Montreal Shamrocks	–
1900	Montreal Shamrocks	–	Halifax Crescents	–
			Winnipeg Victorias	–
1899	Montreal Shamrocks	–	Queens University	–
	Montreal Victorias	–	Winnipeg Victorias	–
1898	Montreal Victorias	–	(no challengers)	
1897	Montreal Victorias	–	Ottawa Capitals	–
1896	Montreal Victorias	–	Winnipeg Victorias	–
	Winnipeg Victorias	–	Montreal Victorias	–
1895	Montreal Victorias	–	(no challengers)	
1894	Montreal AAA	–	Ottawa Generals	–
1893	Montreal AAA	–	(no challengers)	

CONN SMYTHE TROPHY WINNERS

Year	Player	Team		Year	Player	Team
1989	Al MacInnis	Calgary		1976	Reggie Leach	Philadelphia
1988	Wayne Gretzky	Edmonton		1975	Bernie Parent	Philadelphia
1987	Ron Hextall	Philadelphia		1974	Bernie Parent	Philadelphia
1986	Patrick Roy	Montreal		1973	Yvon Cournoyer	Montreal
1985	Wayne Gretzky	Edmonton		1972	Bobby Orr	Boston
1984	Mark Messier	Edmonton		1971	Ken Dryden	Montreal
1983	Bill Smith	NY Islanders		1970	Bobby Orr	Boston
1982	Mike Bossy	NY Islanders		1969	Serge Savard	Montreal
1981	Butch Goring	NY Islanders		1968	Glenn Hall	St. Louis
1980	Bryan Trottier	NY Islanders		1967	Dave Keon	Toronto
1979	Bob Gainey	Montreal		1966	Roger Crozier	Detroit
1978	Larry Robinson	Montreal		1965	Jean Beliveau	Montreal
1977	Guy Lafleur	Montreal				

STANLEY CUP TRUSTEES

INDEX

SELECTED BIBLIOGRAPHY

Boileau, Ron. *The Pacific Coast Hockey Association.*
    Coquitlam, B.C.: 1984. (Manuscript)
Coleman, Charles. *The Trail of the Stanley Cup.* Dubuque,
    Iowa: Kendall/Hunt, 1964. (Vol. 1-3)
Fischler, Stan and Shirley Walton Fischler. *The Hockey
    Encyclopedia.* New York: MacMillan, 1983.
Flood, Brian. *Saint John; A Sporting Tradition 1785-1985.*
    Neptune: Canada, 1985.
The Hockey News Index. Edited by James Duplacey and
    Joseph Romain. Toronto, Ont.: The Hockey Hall of Fame
    and Museum, [198-]. (Manuscript)
McFarlane, Brian. *The Stanley Cup.* Toronto, Ont.:
    Pagurian, [197-].
National Hockey League. *The National Hockey League;
    Official Guide and Record Book 1988-89.* Montreal, Que.:
    National Hockey League, 1988.
1988 Stanley Cup Championship Media Guide. Edited by
    Steven M. Charendoff. [Montreal, Que.]: [National Hockey
    League], [1988]. (Manuscript)
Sweeney, Ed. *Hockey Manitoba 1890 to 1915.* [Manitoba]:
    [Manitoba Sports Hall of Fame], [198-]. (Manuscript)

PICTURE CREDITS

Bruce Bennett Studios: Bruce Bennett 2-3, 6, 7, 10, 11, 93(top), 135(bottom), 146-147(all
    three), 150(bottom), 151, 152, 156(top right, bottom), 157, 158(top), 159(both), 160-
    161(all three), 162-163(both), 164(both), 165, 166-167(both), 168-169(all three), 170-
    171(all three), 172-173(all three), 174-175(all three), 176(both), 178(bottom), 179(all
    three), 180(bottom), 181, 182(both), 184(bottom), 185, 186(both), 187; Melchior DiGia-
    como 14, 15, 118, 120, 128, 129(top), 132(top), 134, 135(top both), 140-141(all three), 142-
    143(all four), 145, 148(right), 149, 153(bottom), 154(both); Joe DiMaggio/Joanne Kalish
    156(top left); Harry Klaff 129(bottom), 130-131.
The Bettmann Archive, Inc.: 21(bottom), 57(bottom), 58(top), 60(top), 61, 63, 64(top).
Brompton Picture Library: 70-71(bottom).
Bill Fitsell: 17(top), 30(top), 38(both).
Hockey Hall of Fame and Museum, Toronto: 8, 9, 12(bottom both), 13, 16(both), 17(bot-
    tom), 18-19(all), 20, 21(top center), 22, 23(both), 24, 25, 26(top, bottom), 27(bottom),
    28, 29(both), 30(bottom), 31(both), 32(left), 33, 34(top), 35, 36-37(all three), 39(both),
    40-41(all three), 42-43(all three), 44, 45, 46-47(all four), 48, 49(bottom), 50(both), 52,
    53(both), 54(right), 55, 57(top), 59, 60(bottom), 62(all three), 65(top) 66(both), 67(bot-
    tom), 68-69(all three), 70(top, bottom left), 72-73(all three), 74(top), 75, 76, 77(top),
    78(top), 79, 80-81(all three), 82-83(all four), 84-85(all three), 87, 88(top), 89(all three),
    90-91(all five), 92(bottom), 93(bottom), 94-95(all three), 96-97(all three), 98-99(all
    three), 100(top), 101(bottom), 103, 105(both), 106-107(all three), 108(both), 109(left),
    110, 112(top), 113, 116-117(all three), 119, 121(both), 124-125(all four), 136-137, 138-139,
    148(top left).
International Hockey Hall of Fame and Museum, Kingston, Ontario: 32(right).
McGill University Archives: 27(top).
Public Archives of Canada: 51(top).
Public Archives of Nova Scotia, Photograph Collection: 12(top).
UPI/Bettmann Newsphotos: 1, 49(top), 51(bottom), 54(left), 56, 58(bottom), 64(bottom),
    65(bottom), 67(top), 74(bottom), 77(bottom), 78(bottom), 86(both), 88(both), 92(top),
    100(bottom), 101(top), 102(both), 104(both), 109(right), 111, 112(bottom), 114-115(both),
    122-123, 126-127(all three), 132(bottom), 133, 144, 148(bottom left), 150(top), 153(top),
    155, 158(bottom), 164(top), 1/7(both), 178(top), 180(top), 183(both), 184(top).

ACKNOWLEDGEMENTS

Several people need to be identified as invaluable to the authors. Charles
Coleman spent much of his life producing a three-volume work called *The
Trail of the Stanley Cup*, the most valuable reference tool in the field of
hockey research, without which the preparation of this book would have been
impossible. Steve Charendoff of the NHL Public Relations Department produced a remarkable historical guide to the Stanley Cup playoffs, which we
consulted regularly. Lefty Reid, Scotty Morrison, and their staff at the Hockey
Hall of Fame were helpful and supportive of this effort; Tom Gaston and
Nicola Murray, and Sid Shapira of the Library Department at the Hall were in-
dispensable; and Dan Diamond, as always, proved a loyal and useful re-
source.

The authors and publisher would also like to thank the following people who
helped in the preparation of this book: Mike Rose, designer, Rita Longabucco,
picture editor; Jean Martin, editor; and Elizabeth A. McCarthy, indexer.